HEINEMANN MODULAR MATHEMATICS
for
LONDON AS AND A-LEVEL
Mechanics 3

John Hebborn   Jean Littlewood

1

2

3

4

D1380012

Heinemann Educational Publishers
Halley Court, Jordan Hill, Oxford, OX2 8EJ
a division of Reed Educational & Professional Publishing Ltd

MELBOURNE AUCKLAND FLORENCE PRAGUE
MADRID ATHENS SINGAPORE TOKYO
SÃO PAULO CHICAGO PORTSMOUTH (NH)
MEXICO CITY IBADAN GABORONE JOHANNESBURG
KAMPALA NAIROBI

© John Hebborn and Jean Littlewood 1996

All rights reserved. No part of this publication may be reproduced, stored in a
retrieval system, or transmitted in any form or by any means, electronic,
mechanical, photocopying, recording, or otherwise without either the prior
written permission of the Publishers or a licence permitting restricted copying in
the United Kingdom issued by the Copyright Licensing Agency Ltd,
90 Tottenham Court Road, London W1P 9HE.

First published 1996

98 10 9 8 7 6 5 4 3

ISBN 0 435518054

Original design by Geoffrey Wadsley: additional design work by Jim Turner

Typeset by Keyword Typesetting Services Limited, Wallington, Surrey

Printed in Great Britain by The Bath Press, Bath

Acknowledgements:

The publisher's and authors' thanks are due to Edexcel Foundation for
permission to reproduce questions from past examination papers. These are
marked with an [L].
  The answers have been provided by the authors and are not the responsibility
of the examining board.

About this book

This book is designed to provide you with the best preparation possible for your London Modular Mathematics M3 examination. The series authors are examiners and exam moderators themselves and have a good understanding of the exam board's requirements.

Finding your way around

To help to find your way around when you are studying and revising use the:

- **edge marks** (shown on the front page) – these help you to get to the right chapter quickly;
- **contents list** – this lists the headings that identify key syllabus ideas covered in the book so you can turn straight to them;
- **index** – if you need to find a topic the **bold** number shows where to find the main entry on a topic.

Remembering key ideas

We have provided clear explanations of the key ideas and techniques you need throughout the book. Key ideas you need to remember are listed in a **summary of key points** at the end of each chapter and are marked like this in the chapters:

- ■ **work done** $= \displaystyle\int_{x_1}^{x_2} F(x)\,dx$

Exercises and exam questions

In this book questions are carefully graded so they increase in difficulty and gradually bring you up to exam standard.

- **past exam questions** are marked with an L;
- **review exercises** on pages **59** and **137** help you practise answering questions from several areas of mathematics at once, as in the real exam;
- **examination style practice paper** – this is designed to help you prepare for the exam itself;
- **answers** are included at the end of the book – use them to check your work.

Contents

A knowledge and expertise in the contents of Books M1 and M2, chapters 8 and 9 of Book P2, together with a knowledge of integration and differential equations as in chapters 5 and 8 of Book P3 is assumed and expected.

Moments of inertia of a rigid body

In Book M2 the motion of a particle moving in a circle was studied. When a body cannot be modelled as a particle the study of its rotational motion is more complicated.

1.1   What is a moment of inertia?

The **inertia** of a particle or larger body is a measure of its reluctance to move. For a body which can be modelled as a particle the mass of the body determines its inertia. For a larger body which is rotating about a fixed axis the particle model is no longer appropriate and its reluctance to move is determined by a quantity called its **moment of inertia**.

Consider a lamina which is rotating about a fixed axis which passes through a point O of the lamina and is perpendicular to the plane of the lamina.

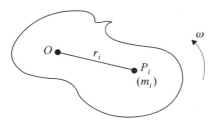

Think of the lamina as being composed of particles $P_1, P_2, \ldots, P_n$ of masses $m_1, m_2, \ldots, m_n$ which are at distances $r_1, r_2, \ldots, r_n$ from the axis. Each of the radius vectors $OP_1, OP_2, \ldots, OP_n$ will be rotating with the same angular speed ω, commonly referred to as the angular speed of the lamina. A typical particle P_i of mass m_i is shown in the diagram. This particle has a linear speed $r_i\omega$ (Book M2, chapter 3) and so its kinetic energy is

$$\tfrac{1}{2}m_i(r_i\omega)^2 = \tfrac{1}{2}m_i r_i^2 \omega^2$$

The total kinetic energy of the lamina is obtained by summing over all the particles. This gives:

$$\text{K.E. of lamina} = \tfrac{1}{2}m_1\,r_1^2\,\omega^2 + \tfrac{1}{2}m_2\,r_2^2\,\omega^2 + \ldots + \tfrac{1}{2}m_n\,r_n^2\,\omega^2$$
$$= \tfrac{1}{2}\omega^2(m_1\,r_1^2 + m_2\,r_2^2 + \ldots + m_n\,r_n^2)$$

The quantity $(m_1r_1^2 + m_2r_2^2 + \ldots + m_nr_n^2)$ depends only on how the mass of the lamina is distributed relative to the axis of rotation. It is called the **moment of inertia** of the lamina about this axis.

If you consider the kinetic energy of a three-dimensional rotating body in the same way, you will get the same result.

■   **The moment of inertia (M.I.) of a rigid body about an axis is**

$$\sum_i m_i r_i^2 \quad \textbf{where } m_i \textbf{ is the mass of a typical particle and } r_i \textbf{ is the}$$

distance of that particle from the axis.

The symbol I is usually used for moment of inertia. When the mass of a body is measured in kilograms and distances in metres, the moment of inertia of the body is measured in $\text{kg}\,\text{m}^2$.

Note that since the moment of inertia of a body about an axis depends on the distances of the separate particles from that axis, it is meaningless to talk about the moment of inertia of a body without stating the axis of rotation.

The moment of inertia of a body about a given axis is a measure of its reluctance to turn about that axis. The larger the moment of inertia the harder it is to change the angular speed of the body. The definition of the moment of inertia of a body about a given axis is the same for *all* bodies. However, in the following work we will only be considering objects which can be modelled as rigid bodies, as defined in Book M1, chapter 1.

1.2 Calculating moments of inertia

The method of calculating the moment of inertia of a body about a given axis is similar to the method of calculating the position of the centre of mass of a body (Book M2, chapter 6). Sometimes $\sum_i m_i r_i^2$ can be found by straightforward summation but in other cases the summation will lead to integration.

Example 1

Find the moment of inertia of a circular hoop of mass M and radius a about an axis through its centre perpendicular to its plane.

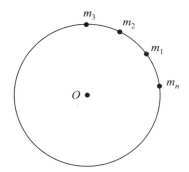

Think of the hoop as composed of a set of particles of masses $m_1, m_2, \ldots, m_n$ where $m_1 + m_2 + \ldots + m_n = M$, all at the same distance a from the centre O of the hoop and hence all at the same distance a from the axis.

So: moment of inertia $= \displaystyle\sum_i m_i a^2$

$$= m_1 a^2 + m_2 a^2 + \ldots + m_n a^2$$

$$= a^2(m_1 + m_2 + \ldots + m_n)$$

$$= M a^2$$

The particles do not have to be of equal mass and so the result does not depend on the hoop being uniform.

Example 2

Find the moment of inertia of a uniform rod of mass m and length $2a$ about an axis through its centre perpendicular to its length.

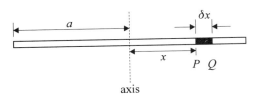

Consider the rod to be composed of small pieces. One such piece, PQ of length δx, at a distance x from the axis, is shown shaded in the diagram. As the rod has mass m and length $2a$ its mass per unit length is $\dfrac{m}{2a}$. So the mass of the small piece PQ is $\dfrac{m}{2a}\,\delta x$.

For this piece: $mr^2 = \left(\dfrac{m}{2a}\,\delta x\right)x^2$

So for the whole rod:

$$\text{moment of inertia} = \sum mr^2$$

$$= \sum_{x=-a}^{x=a} \frac{mx^2}{2a} \, \delta x$$

If you let $\delta x \to 0$ then:

$$\text{moment of inertia} = \lim_{\delta x \to 0} \sum_{x=-a}^{x=a} \frac{mx^2}{2a} \, \delta x$$

$$= \int_{-a}^{a} \frac{mx^2}{2a} \, dx$$

$$= \left[\frac{mx^3}{3 \times 2a} \right]_{-a}^{a}$$

$$= \frac{ma^3}{6a} - \frac{m(-a)^3}{6a}$$

$$= \frac{ma^3}{6a} + \frac{ma^3}{6a}$$

$$= \tfrac{1}{3}ma^2$$

So the required moment of inertia is $\tfrac{1}{3}ma^2$.

Example 3

Find the moment of inertia of a uniform circular disc of mass m and radius r about an axis through its centre O perpendicular to its plane.

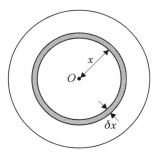

Consider the disc to be composed of a set of concentric hoops, centre O. Let a typical one have width δx and internal radius x as shown shaded in the diagram.

The external radius of the hoop is $x + \delta x$. So:

$$\text{area of the hoop} = \pi(x + \delta x)^2 - \pi x^2$$

$$= 2\pi x \delta x + \pi(\delta x)^2$$

As δx is small, $(\delta x)^2$ can be ignored compared with δx.

So: area of the hoop $= 2\pi x \delta x$

The mass per unit area of the disc is $\dfrac{m}{\pi r^2}$.

So: mass of the hoop $= \left(\dfrac{m}{\pi r^2}\right) 2\pi x \, \delta x$

$$= \dfrac{2mx}{r^2} \, \delta x$$

Using the formula

M.I. of a hoop $=$ mass $\times$ radius^2

as found in example 1,

M.I. of the typical hoop $= \left(\dfrac{2mx}{r^2} \, \delta x\right) \times x^2$

$$= \dfrac{2mx^3}{r^2} \, \delta x$$

And so for the disc:

$$\text{M.I.} = \sum_{x=0}^{x=r} \dfrac{2mx^3}{r^2} \, \delta x$$

Letting $\delta x \to 0$

$$\text{M.I.} = \int_0^r \dfrac{2mx^3}{r^2} \, \mathrm{d}x$$

$$= \left[\dfrac{2mx^4}{4r^2}\right]_0^r$$

$$= \dfrac{2mr^4}{4r^2}$$

$$= \tfrac{1}{2} mr^2$$

1.3 The additive rule

You can deduce many moments of inertia from a few standard results by using various general rules. The first such rule is called the **additive rule** and is readily obtained from the basic definition of moment of inertia.

Suppose two bodies have moments of inertia I_1 and I_2 about the same axis. The first body can be considered to be composed of particles of mass $m_1, m_2, \ldots, m_k$ at distances $r_1, r_2, \ldots, r_k$ from the axis and the second body to be composed of particles of mass $m_{k+1}, m_{k+2}, \ldots, m_n$ at distances $r_{k+1}, r_{k+2}, \ldots, r_n$ from the axis.

So:

$$I_1 = m_1 r_1^2 + m_2 r_2^2 + \ldots + m_k r_k^2$$

and

$$I_2 = m_{k+1} r_{k+1}^2 + m_{k+2} r_{k+2}^2 + \ldots + m_n r_n^2$$

The moment of inertia of the composite body about this axis is

$$m_1 r_1^2 + m_2 r_2^2 + \ldots + m_k r_k^2 + m_{k+1} r_{k+1}^2 + \ldots + m_n r_n^2 = I_1 + I_2$$

Which gives us the **additive rule**:

■ **If two bodies have moments of inertia I_1 and I_2 about the same axis then the M.I. of the composite body about the same axis is $I_1 + I_2$.**

Example 4

A uniform rod AB of length $2a$ and mass m has a particle of mass $2m$ attached to the point C of the rod where $BC = \dfrac{a}{2}$. Calculate the moment of inertia of the rod with the mass attached, about an axis through the mid-point of AB and perpendicular to AB.

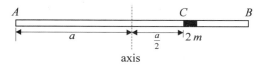

The standard result for the moment of inertia of a rod of length $2a$ and mass m about an axis through its mid-point perpendicular to its length is

$$\text{M.I. of rod} = \tfrac{1}{3}ma^2$$

(see example 2).

The moment of inertia of a particle of mass $2m$, distance $\dfrac{a}{2}$ from the axis, is

$$2m\left(\frac{a}{2}\right)^2 = \tfrac{1}{2}ma^2$$

By the additive rule:

$$\begin{aligned}
\text{M.I. of (rod + particle)} &= \text{M.I. of rod} + \text{M.I. of particle} \\
&= \tfrac{1}{3}ma^2 + \tfrac{1}{2}ma^2 \\
&= ma^2(\tfrac{1}{3} + \tfrac{1}{2}) \\
&= \tfrac{5}{6}ma^2
\end{aligned}$$

Example 5

A uniform ring of mass m is made from a circle of radius a, by cutting out a concentric circle of radius b. This ring, or *annulus*, D_1, is stuck to another uniform disc, D_2, of radius a and mass $2m$ so that the outer circumferences coincide. Show that the moment of inertia of the resulting flywheel about an axis perpendicular to the flywheel and through the centre O of the circles is $\frac{1}{2}m(3a^2 + b^2)$.

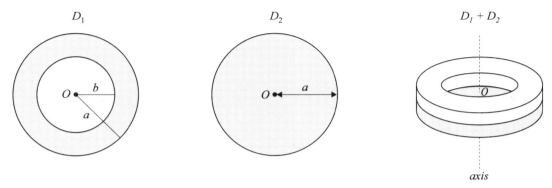

You can think of the flywheel as a uniform disc of radius a plus a second uniform disc of radius a minus a uniform disc of radius b, all having the same centre but different masses.

First consider the disc D_1 which is an annulus of internal radius b, external radius a and mass m.

$$\text{Area of annulus } D_1 = \pi a^2 - \pi b^2 = \pi(a^2 - b^2)$$

So: $$\text{mass per unit area of } D_1 = \frac{m}{\pi(a^2 - b^2)}$$

So the mass of the circular disc, radius a, from which D_1 was cut is

$$\frac{\pi a^2 m}{\pi(a^2 - b^2)} = \frac{ma^2}{a^2 - b^2}$$

The moment of inertia of this circular disc of radius a about a perpendicular axis through its centre is

$$\tfrac{1}{2} \times \text{mass} \times (\text{radius})^2$$

$$= \tfrac{1}{2}\frac{ma^2}{a^2 - b^2} \times a^2$$

$$= \tfrac{1}{2}\frac{ma^4}{a^2 - b^2}$$

Similarly, the moment of inertia of a circular disc of radius b about a perpendicular axis through its centre is $\tfrac{1}{2}\dfrac{mb^4}{a^2 - b^2}$.

By the additive rule:

M.I. of annulus D_1 about a perpendicular axis through its centre

= M.I. of circular disc radius a – M.I. of circular disc radius b, both about the same axis

$$= \tfrac{1}{2} \frac{ma^4}{a^2 - b^2} - \tfrac{1}{2} \frac{mb^4}{a^2 - b^2}$$

$$= \tfrac{1}{2} m \frac{(a^4 - b^4)}{a^2 - b^2}$$

$$= \tfrac{1}{2} m \frac{(a^2 - b^2)(a^2 + b^2)}{a^2 - b^2}$$

$$= \tfrac{1}{2} m (a^2 + b^2)$$

M.I of disc D_2, radius a, mass $2m$ about a perpendicular axis through its centre $= \tfrac{1}{2} \times 2ma^2 = ma^2$

By the additive rule:

M.I. of flywheel about given axis

= M.I. of annulus D_1 + M.I. of disc D_2 about given axis

$$= \tfrac{1}{2} m (a^2 + b^2) + ma^2$$

$$= \tfrac{1}{2} m (3a^2 + b^2)$$

1.4 Using standard results

There are certain standard results for moments of inertia that you are given in the formula book for the examination. You can use these formulae, without proof, to work out other moments of inertia. Here are the three standard results which were derived in examples 1, 2 and 3:

Body	Axis	M.I.
■ Uniform rod, mass m, length $2a$	through centre, perpendicular to rod	$\tfrac{1}{3} ma^2$
■ Circular hoop, mass m, radius r	through centre, perpendicular to plane of hoop	mr^2
■ Uniform circular disc, mass m, radius r	through centre, perpendicular to disc	$\tfrac{1}{2} mr^2$

1.5 The stretching rule

The moment of inertia of a uniform rectangular lamina

Suppose you want to calculate the moment of inertia of a uniform rectangular lamina of mass m and sides $2a$ and $2b$ about an axis joining the mid-points of the sides of length $2a$. Think of the lamina as being composed of strips.

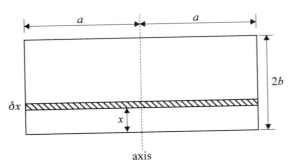

Let a typical strip have width δx and be distant x from a side of length $2a$ of the rectangle. This strip is shown shaded in the diagram.

$$\text{Mass per unit area of lamina} = \frac{m}{2a \times 2b} = \frac{m}{4ab}$$

So: $$\text{mass of strip} = 2a\,\delta x \times \frac{m}{4ab} = \frac{m}{2b}\,\delta x$$

The moment of inertia of the strip about the given axis is the moment of inertia of a rod of length $2a$ about an axis through its centre perpendicular to its length. So:

$$\text{M.I.} = \tfrac{1}{3} \times \text{mass} \times a^2 = \tfrac{1}{3}\left(\frac{m}{2b}\,\delta x\right)a^2 = \tfrac{1}{6}\frac{ma^2}{b}\,\delta x$$

Adding all the strips together and letting $\delta x \to 0$ gives:

$$\text{M.I. of rectangle about given axis} = \int_0^{2b} \frac{ma^2}{6b}\,\mathrm{d}x$$
$$= \frac{ma^2}{6b}\int_0^{2b}\,\mathrm{d}x$$
$$= \frac{ma^2}{6b}\Big[x\Big]_0^{2b}$$
$$= \frac{ma^2}{6b} \times 2b$$
$$= \tfrac{1}{3}ma^2$$

So the moment of inertia of the rectangle is the same as the moment of inertia of a rod of the same mass and length $2a$ about an axis through its centre perpendicular to its length. This is an example of **the stretching rule**:

- **If one body can be obtained from another body by 'stretching' parallel to the axis without altering the distribution of mass *relative to the axis* then the moments of inertia of the two bodies about the axis are the same.**

The moment of inertia of a hollow cylinder

Another body which can be obtained by stretching is a cylinder.

Example 6

A hollow uniform circular cylinder of mass m and base radius a is open at both ends. Calculate the moment of inertia of the cylinder about its axis.

You can think of the cylinder as a 'stretch' of a circular hoop of mass m and radius a along an axis through the centre of the hoop and perpendicular to the plane of the hoop.

Thus: M.I of cylinder about its axis

= M.I. of hoop about perpendicular axis through the centre

$= ma^2$

The same method can be used to calculate the moment of inertia of a solid cylinder about its axis.

1.6   Radius of gyration

Suppose a body of mass m has a moment of inertia I about a given axis of rotation. A particle also of mass m placed at a distance k from the same axis will have moment of inertia mk^2 about that axis. The value of k which makes these two moments of inertia equal is called the **radius of gyration** of the original body about this axis.

The radius of gyration k is given by:

$$I = mk^2$$

or

$$k = \sqrt{\left(\frac{I}{m}\right)}$$

Example 7

Calculate the radius of gyration of a rod of mass m and length $2a$ about an axis through its centre, perpendicular to its length

M.I. of rod about given axis $= \frac{1}{3}ma^2$

Let the radius of gyration be k.

Then:

$$k = \sqrt{\left(\frac{I}{m}\right)} = \sqrt{(\tfrac{1}{3}a^2)}$$

so:

$$k = \frac{a\sqrt{3}}{3}$$

Exercise 1A

In questions 1–5, use integration to calculate the moments of inertia and radii of gyration of the bodies about the given axes.

1 A uniform rod of mass m and length $2a$ about an axis through one end, perpendicular to its length.

2 A uniform rod of mass m and length l about an axis perpendicular to its length through a point distant a from one end.

3 A uniform rod of mass m and length l about an axis through one end inclined at an angle θ to the rod.

4 A uniform triangular lamina of mass m in the shape of an isosceles triangle with base $2b$ and height h, about its axis of symmetry.

5 A uniform lamina of mass m bounded by the curve with equation $y^2 = 4ax$ and the line $x = 4a$ about the x-axis.

In questions 6–14 use standard results (see the table at the end of this chapter) to calculate the required moments of inertia.

6 A circular hoop of mass m and radius r, with three particles of masses m, $2m$ and $3m$ attached to points on the hoop, about an axis through its centre.

7 A uniform rod of length l and mass m, about an axis through one end perpendicular to its length. (Hint: consider the rod to be half of a rod of length $2l$ and mass $2m$.)

8 A uniform rectangular lamina of mass m and sides l and b, about an axis through the mid-points of the sides of length l.

9 A uniform rod of mass m and length $2a$ with a particle of mass $2m$ attached to a point distant $\dfrac{a}{3}$ from one end, about an axis through its mid-point perpendicular to its length.

10 A uniform circular disc mass m and diameter d with particles of masses m, $2m$ and $4m$ attached at points distance $\dfrac{d}{3}$, $\dfrac{d}{3}$ and $\dfrac{d}{6}$ respectively from the centre, about a perpendicular axis through its centre.

11 An equilateral triangle ABC is formed by joining three light rods of length l. Particles of masses m, $2m$ and $3m$, are attached to the triangle at the mid-points of AB, BC and AC respectively. Calculate the moment of inertia of the system about an axis through A perpendicular to the plane of the triangle.

12 Calculate the moment of inertia of a uniform, hollow, closed cylinder of mass M, base radius r and height h, about its axis.

13 A uniform lamina of mass m is formed from a square lamina of side $2a$ by cutting away a square of side $2b$. Both squares have the same centre and their sides are parallel as shown. A and B are the mid-points of opposite sides of the lamina. Calculate the moment of inertia of the lamina about AB.

14 Calculate the moment of inertia of a uniform solid cylinder of mass M, base radius r and height h about its axis.

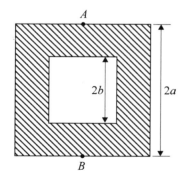

1.7 Moments of inertia of spheres

Using the additive rule and integration allows you to calculate the moments of inertia of more complicated bodies.

Moment of inertia of a solid sphere

Example 8

Find the moment of inertia of a uniform solid sphere of mass m and radius r about an axis coinciding with a diameter.

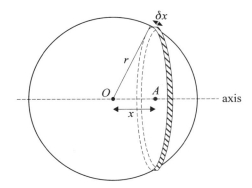

Consider the sphere to be composed of discs whose planes are perpendicular to the axis. Let a typical disc have thickness δx, be distant x from the centre O of the sphere and have centre A, as shown shaded in the diagram. By Pythagoras' theorem, the radius of the disc is $\sqrt{(r^2 - x^2)}$.

So: volume of disc $= \pi(r^2 - x^2)\delta x$

The mass per unit volume of the sphere is

$$\frac{m}{\frac{4}{3}\pi r^3} = \frac{3m}{4\pi r^3}$$

So: mass of disc $= \pi(r^2 - x^2)\,\delta x \times \dfrac{3m}{4\pi r^3}$

$$= \frac{3m(r^2 - x^2)\,\delta x}{4r^3}$$

The axis passes through the centre of the disc and is perpendicular to the disc.

So: $\text{M.I. of disc} = \frac{1}{2} \times \text{mass} \times \text{radius}^2$

$$= \frac{1}{2} \times \frac{3m(r^2 - x^2)}{4r^3} \times (r^2 - x^2)\, \delta x$$

$$= \frac{3m}{8r^3} (r^2 - x^2)^2 \, \delta x$$

Adding the moments of inertia of the separate discs and letting $\delta x \to 0$ gives:

$\text{M.I. of sphere about given axis} = \displaystyle\int_{-r}^{r} \frac{3m}{8r^3} (r^2 - x^2)^2 \, dx$

$$= \frac{3m}{8r^3} \int_{-r}^{r} (r^4 - 2r^2 x^2 + x^4) \, dx$$

$$= \frac{3m}{8r^3} \left[r^4 x - \frac{2r^2 x^3}{3} + \frac{x^5}{5} \right]_{-r}^{r}$$

$$= \frac{3m}{8r^3} \left[r^5 - \frac{2r^5}{3} + \frac{r^5}{5} - \left(-r^5 + \frac{2r^5}{3} - \frac{r^5}{5} \right) \right]$$

$$= \frac{3m}{8r^3} \times 2 \times \frac{8r^5}{15}$$

$$= \frac{2}{5} mr^2$$

■ **So the moment of inertia of a uniform solid sphere of mass m and radius r about an axis coinciding with a diameter is $\frac{2}{5} mr^2$.**

The moment of inertia of a solid cone about its axis can be found in the same way.

Moment of inertia of a hollow sphere

To calculate the moment of inertia of a hollow sphere about an axis which coincides with a diameter, think of the sphere as a set of hoops. However, if you use slightly different radii for the two circles bounding each hoop, the surface of each hoop is slightly sloped and fits more closely to the actual surface of the sphere. This provides a closer approximation to the surface area and hence the mass of the sphere than can be obtained using 'straight' sided hoops. Let the sphere have mass m and radius r.

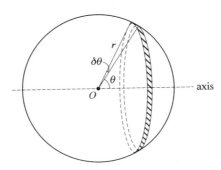

A typical hoop with planes perpendicular to the axis is shown in this diagram.

Let the angle between the axis and the radius of the sphere which joins a point on the outer circular boundary of the hoop to the centre of the sphere be θ as shown. The angle between the axis and the radius of the sphere which joins a point on the inner circular boundary will be $\theta + \delta\theta$.

Each hoop is approximately a hollow cylinder. The centre of the hoop is on the axis of rotation, its radius is $r\sin\theta$ and its width is $r\,\delta\theta$.

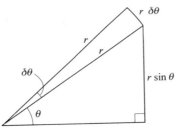

So: surface area of hoop $= 2\pi r \sin\theta \times r\delta\theta$

Surface area of sphere $= 4\pi r^2$

So: mass per unit area of sphere $= \dfrac{m}{4\pi r^2}$

And so: mass of hoop $= 2\pi r^2 \sin\theta \times \dfrac{m}{4\pi r^2}\,\delta\theta$

$$= \frac{m\sin\theta}{2}\,\delta\theta$$

M.I. of hoop about perpendicular axis through centre

$$= \text{mass} \times \text{radius}^2$$

$$= \frac{m\sin\theta}{2}\,r^2\sin^2\theta\,\delta\theta$$

Adding the moments of inertia of the separate hoops and letting $\delta\theta \to 0$ gives:

M.I. of sphere about a diameter $= \displaystyle\int_0^\pi \frac{mr^2}{2} \sin\theta \,.\, \sin^2\theta \,\mathrm{d}\theta$

$$= \frac{mr^2}{2} \int_0^\pi \sin\theta(1 - \cos^2\theta)\,\mathrm{d}\theta$$

using $\sin^2\theta + \cos^2\theta \equiv 1$

$$= \frac{mr^2}{2} \int_0^\pi (\sin\theta - \sin\theta\cos^2\theta)\,\mathrm{d}\theta$$

$$= \frac{mr^2}{2} \left[-\cos\theta + \tfrac{1}{3}\cos^3\theta \right]_0^\pi$$

$$= \frac{mr^2}{2} [-(-1) + \tfrac{1}{3}(-1)^3 - (-1 + \tfrac{1}{3})]$$

$$= \frac{mr^2}{2} [1 - \tfrac{1}{3} + 1 - \tfrac{1}{3}]$$

$$= \frac{mr^2}{2} \times \tfrac{4}{3}$$

$$= \frac{2mr^2}{3}$$

- **So the moment of inertia of a hollow sphere of mass m and radius r about a diameter is $\dfrac{2mr^2}{3}$.**

1.8   The parallel axis theorem

Most of the moments of inertia found so far have been about an axis which passes through the centre of mass of the body. If you know the moment of inertia of a body about such an axis, you can calculate the moment of inertia of that body about *any* parallel axis by using the **parallel axis theorem**:

- **If the moment of inertia of a body of mass m about an axis through its centre of mass, G, is I_G then the moment of inertia about any axis parallel to the original axis and distant d from it is $I_G + md^2$.**

To prove this theorem, consider a body of mass M and let AB be the axis through the centre of mass G. Let $A'B'$ be an axis parallel to AB and distance d from AB.

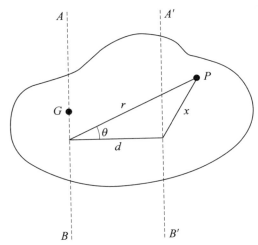

Consider a particle P of mass m which is a distance x from $A'B'$ and a distance r from AB.

By the cosine rule (Book P2, chapter 7):

$$x^2 = d^2 + r^2 - 2dr \cos \theta$$

and so the moment of inertia of P about $A'B'$ is

$$mx^2 = m(d^2 + r^2 - 2dr \cos \theta)$$

So the moment of inertia of the body about $A'B'$ is

$$\Sigma mx^2 = \Sigma m(d^2 + r^2 - 2dr \cos \theta)$$
$$= d^2 \Sigma m + \Sigma mr^2 - 2d\Sigma mr \cos \theta$$

Now $$\Sigma m = M \quad \text{and} \quad \Sigma mr^2 = I_G$$

But: $\quad mr \cos \theta = $ moment of mass of P about AB

and since AB passes through the centre of mass of the body

$$\Sigma mr \cos \theta = 0$$

(Book M1, chapter 6). So the moment of inertia of the body about $A'B'$ is

$$I_G + Md^2$$

Example 9

Find the moment of inertia of a uniform hoop of radius a and mass m about an axis through a point A of the hoop perpendicular to the plane of the hoop.

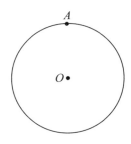

The moment of inertia of a hoop about an axis through its centre O perpendicular to the plane of the hoop is ma^2. Let A be any point on the hoop. Then $OA = a$ and by the parallel axis theorem:

M.I of hoop about axis through A perpendicular to plane of hoop

$$= \text{M.I. of hoop about parallel axis through } O + ma^2$$
$$= ma^2 + ma^2$$
$$= 2ma^2$$

If the moment of inertia of a body about *any axis* is given, then you can calculate the moment of inertia about *any other parallel axis*, as long as you know the distances of each axis from the centre of mass. The calculation must be performed in two stages, as shown in the next example.

Example 10

A uniform equilateral triangular lamina ABC of mass m has $AB = AC = BC = l$. The moment of inertia of the lamina about an axis through A perpendicular to its plane is $\frac{5}{12}ml^2$. Calculate the moment of inertia of the lamina about a parallel axis through D, the mid-point of BC.

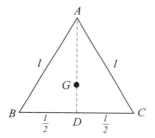

The centre of mass of the lamina is at G, where $GD = \frac{1}{3}AD$ (Book M1, section 6.4). Hence by Pythagoras' Theorem in $\triangle ACD$,

$$GD = \frac{1}{3}\sqrt{\left(l^2 - \frac{l^2}{4}\right)} = \frac{1}{3}\sqrt{\left(\frac{3l^2}{4}\right)} = \frac{l\sqrt{3}}{6}$$

and so
$$AG = 2GD = \frac{l\sqrt{3}}{3}$$

By the parallel axis theorem:

M.I. about given axis through A =
M.I. about parallel axis through $G + m \times (AG)^2$

So: M.I. about axis through $G = \frac{5}{12}ml^2 - m \times \frac{3l^2}{9}$

$$= \frac{5}{12}ml^2 - \frac{1}{3}ml^2 = \frac{1}{12}ml^2$$

M.I. about parallel axis through D

$$= \text{M.I. about axis through } G + m \times (GD)^2$$

$$= \tfrac{1}{12}ml^2 + m \times \frac{3l^2}{36}$$

$$= \tfrac{1}{6}ml^2$$

1.9 The perpendicular axes theorem for a lamina

When you know the moments of inertia of a lamina about two perpendicular axes Ox and Oy in the plane of the lamina, you can find the moment of inertia of the lamina about the axis through O perpendicular to the plane of the lamina by adding these two moments of inertia.

Consider a plane lamina which is composed of particles P_i of mass m_i situated at points with coordinates (x_i, y_i) relative to the axes Ox and Oy. The axes are fixed in the plane of the lamina.

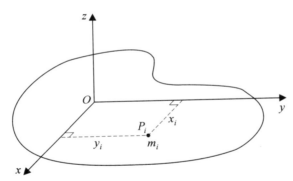

Suppose the moments of inertia of the lamina about the axes Ox and Oy are I_x and I_y respectively.

Then:
$$I_x = \Sigma m_i y_i^2$$

and
$$I_y = \Sigma m_i x_i^2$$

So:
$$I_x + I_y = \Sigma m_i y_i^2 + \Sigma m_i x_i^2$$
$$= \Sigma m_i (x_i^2 + y_i^2)$$

But
$$(x_i^2 + y_i^2) = (\text{distance of } P_i \text{ from } O)^2$$
$$= (\text{distance of } P_i \text{ from } Oz)^2$$

Hence: $I_x + I_y = \Sigma m_i \, (\text{distance of } P_i \text{ from } Oz)^2$

That is: $I_x + I_y = I_z$

This is the **perpendicular axes theorem for a lamina**:

■ **Where I_x, I_y are the moments of inertia of the lamina about two perpendicular axes Ox and Oy in the plane of the lamina and I_z is the moment of inertia of the lamina about the mutually perpendicular axis Oz,**

$$I_x + I_y = I_z$$

Remember that the perpendicular axes theorem applies to *laminae* only.

Example 11

Find the moment of inertia of a uniform rectangular lamina of mass m and sides $2a$, $2b$ about

(a) an axis through its centre G, perpendicular to its plane

(b) an axis through a corner, perpendicular to its plane.

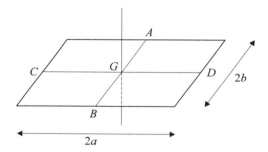

(a) By the stretching rule (page 9) the moment of inertia of a rectangular lamina about an axis joining the mid-points of opposite sides is the same as the moment of inertia of a rod of the same mass and length, along an axis through its centre perpendicular to its length.

So: M.I. of rectangle about $AB = \frac{1}{3}ma^2$

and: M.I. of rectangle about $CD = \frac{1}{3}mb^2$

Hence, by the perpendicular axes theorem, M.I. of rectangle about the perpendicular axis through its centre, G, is

$$\tfrac{1}{3}m(a^2 + b^2)$$

(b) An axis through a corner perpendicular to the plane of the lamina is parallel to the axis through its centre G perpendicular to its plane. (This axis passes through the centre of mass of the lamina.)

The distance, d, from the centre to a corner is $\sqrt{(a^2 + b^2)}$. So, by the parallel axis theorem,

M.I. about perpendicular axis through a corner

$= $ M.I. about the parallel axis through G, the

centre of mass $+ md^2$

$= \frac{1}{3}m(a^2 + b^2) + m(a^2 + b^2)$

$= \frac{4}{3}m(a^2 + b^2)$

Example 12

A uniform cuboid of mass m has edges of length l, b and h. Calculate the moment of inertia of the cuboid about an edge of length h.

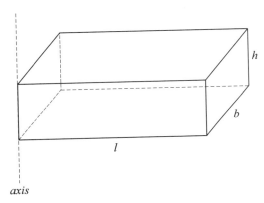

The cuboid can be obtained by stretching a rectangular lamina of sides l, b along an axis through a corner, perpendicular to its plane. The moment of inertia of such a lamina about this axis is, by the result of example 11:

$$\frac{4}{3}m\left[\left(\frac{l}{2}\right)^2 + \left(\frac{b}{2}\right)^2\right] = \frac{1}{3}m(l^2 + b^2)$$

So the moment of inertia of the cuboid about the side of length h is $\frac{1}{3}m(l^2 + b^2)$.

Exercise 1B

1 Find, by integration, the moment of inertia of a uniform solid cone of base radius r, height h and mass m about its axis of symmetry.

2 Find the moment of inertia of a uniform circular disc of mass m and radius r about an axis through a point on the rim perpendicular to the plane of the disc.

3 Find the moment of inertia of a uniform disc of mass m and radius r about a diameter. Hence find the moment of inertia of the disc about a tangent.

4 Find the moment of inertia of a uniform rod of length $2a$ and mass m about an axis parallel to the rod and at a distance d from the rod.

5 A uniform square framework is formed by joining four rods of length $2a$ and mass m. Find the moment of inertia of the framework (a) about an axis through the centre perpendicular to the plane of the framework (b) about an axis through one corner perpendicular to the plane of the framework (c) about an axis through the mid-point of a side perpendicular to the plane of the framework.

6 A uniform rod of length $2r$ and mass $2m$ has two uniform circular discs of mass m and radius r attached one at each end so that the rod lies in the plane of the discs as shown.

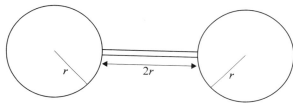

The rod lies along the line of centres of the two discs. Find the moment of inertia of the combined body:

(a) about an axis through the mid-point of the rod perpendicular to the plane of the body

(b) about an axis through one end of the rod perpendicular to the plane of the body

(c) about an axis through one end of the rod perpendicular to the rod and in the plane of the body

(d) about an axis through a point of trisection of the rod, perpendicular to the rod and in the plane of the body.

7 Find the moment of inertia of a uniform brick of mass m and sides a, b, c about an axis joining the mid-points of two edges of length a of one face of the brick with edges a and c.

8   Find the radius of gyration of a uniform circular disc radius r about an axis through a point on its rim perpendicular to the disc.

9   Show that if a body has a radius of gyration k_G about an axis l through its centre of mass G then its radius of gyration about a parallel axis at a distance d from l is $\sqrt{(k_G^2 + d^2)}$.

10 A uniform solid is formed by rotating the region bounded by the curve $y^2 = 16x$ and the line $x = 4$ through one revolution about the x-axis. Find the radius of gyration of this solid about the x-axis.

11 Find the moment of inertia of a uniform solid sphere of mass m and radius r about a tangent to any point on its surface.

12 A uniform solid is formed by rotating the region bounded by the curve with equation $y = \sin x$ and the x-axis between $x = 0$ and $x = \pi$ through one revolution about the x-axis. Find the radius of gyration of this solid about the x-axis.

13 A flywheel of mass m is made from a uniform circular disc of radius $2a$ by cutting away a concentric circular disc of radius a. Find the moment of inertia of the flywheel (a) about an axis through the centre perpendicular to the flywheel (b) about an axis perpendicular to the flywheel through a point on its outer rim.

14 Find the radius of gyration of a uniform square lamina of mass m and side $2a$ about a diagonal.

SUMMARY OF KEY POINTS

1   The moment of inertia (M.I.) of a rigid body about a given axis is $\displaystyle\sum_i m_i r_i^2$ where m_i is the mass of a typical particle and r_i is the distance of that particle from the axis. Moments of inertia are usually measured in $\text{kg}\,\text{m}^2$.

2   The additive rule:
    If two bodies have moments of inertia I_1 and I_2 about the same axis, then the moment of inertia of the composite body is $I_1 + I_2$.

3 The stretching rule:
  If one body can be obtained from another body of equal mass by stretching parallel to the axis without alteration of the distribution of mass relative to the axis then the moments of inertia of the two bodies are the same.

4 The radius of gyration k of a body of mass m about a specified axis is the distance from the axis at which a particle of equal mass must be placed to have the same moment of inertia I about the axis.

$$I = mk^2$$

5 The parallel axis theorem:
  If the moment of inertia of a body of mass m about an axis through its centre of mass, G, is I_G then the moment of inertia about /any axis parallel to the original axis and distance d from it is $I_G + md^2$.

6 The perpendicular axes theorem:
  When the moments of inertia of a *lamina* about two perpendicular axes in the plane of the lamina are known, then the moment of inertia of the lamina about an axis through their point of intersection perpendicular to the plane of the lamina is the sum of these two moments of inertia.

7 You may quote the following standard results without proof unless you are asked to prove them:

Body	Axis	M.I.
Uniform rod, mass m, length $2a$	through centre, perpendicular to rod	$\frac{1}{3}ma^2$
Circular hoop, mass m, radius r	through centre, perpendicular to plane of hoop	mr^2
Uniform circular disc, mass m, radius r	through centre, perpendicular to disc	$\frac{1}{2}mr^2$
Uniform solid sphere, mass m, radius r	about diameter	$\frac{2}{5}mr^2$

Rotation of a rigid body about a fixed smooth axis

2

If you want to study the motion of a rigid body rotating about a fixed axis, you need to know the moment of inertia of the body about that axis. The methods for calculating moments of inertia have been demonstrated in chapter 1. Now you can study the rotational motion of any rigid body for which you can calculate the moment of inertia about a specified axis. In particular, the table of standard results in the summary of chapter 1 gives the moments of inertia of a uniform rod, a circular hoop or disc and a uniform solid sphere about specified axes. So you can study the rotational motion of bodies that can be modelled as some combination of these solids without any complicated initial calculations of their moments of inertia. Pulley wheels, either solid or in the shape of a hoop with spokes, can be modelled as discs if solid or a combination of rods and a hoop otherwise. A solid cylinder can be obtained from a uniform disc by stretching and a cylindrical shell from a circular hoop, combined with uniform discs if the cylinder is closed. By these means, many rotating bodies can be modelled mathematically.

2.1 The kinetic and potential energies of a rotating body

In chapter 1 the kinetic energy of a rigid body rotating with angular speed ω was found to be $\frac{1}{2}\sum_i m_i r_i^2 \omega^2$. When the moment of inertia, I, of the body is defined to be $\sum_i m_i r_i^2$, this gives

■
$$\textbf{K.E. of body} = \tfrac{1}{2}I\omega^2$$

A rotating body will in general have potential energy as well as kinetic energy. Consider the body to be composed of particles of mass $m_1, m_2, \ldots, m_n$ which are at heights $h_1, h_2, \ldots, h_n$ above some (arbitrary) fixed level.

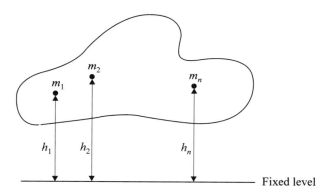

Then, relative to this fixed level, the potential energy of the body is:

$$m_1gh_1 + m_2gh_2 + \ldots + m_ngh_n$$
$$= (m_1h_1 + m_2h_2 + \ldots + m_nh_n)g$$

But

$$m_1h_1 + m_2h_2 + \ldots + m_nh_n = Mh \qquad \text{(Book M1, chapter 6)}$$

where M is the mass of the body and h is the height of the centre of mass of the body above the same fixed level.

So: $\qquad\qquad$ P.E. of body $= Mgh$

■ **When a rigid body is moving, the gain in P.E. of the body is the product of its weight and the vertical height gained by its centre of mass.**

If a rigid body is rotating about a smooth axis and no external forces are acting on the body, the principle of conservation of mechanical energy will hold. That is, the sum of the kinetic and potential energies of the body will remain constant throughout the motion.

Example 1

A uniform circular disc has mass 1 kg and radius 0.5 m. Particles P_1 and P_2 of mass 0.2 kg and 0.5 kg respectively are attached to the disc at distances 0.1 m and 0.3 m respectively from the centre O of the disc. The disc is rotating in a horizontal plane about a smooth vertical axis through its centre O. Calculate the kinetic energy of the system when the disc is rotating at 5 rad s^{-1}.

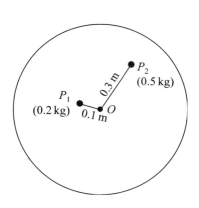

By the additive rule:

M.I. of system, $I = (\frac{1}{2} \times 1 \times 0.5^2 + 0.2 \times 0.1^2 + 0.5 \times 0.3^2)\,\text{kg m}^2$
$$= 0.172\,\text{kg m}^2$$

$$\text{K.E. of system} = \tfrac{1}{2}I\omega^2 = \tfrac{1}{2} \times 0.172 \times 5^2 \, \text{J}$$
$$= 2.15 \, \text{J}$$

The kinetic energy of the disc and particles is 2.15 J.

Example 2

A uniform rod AB of length 1 m and mass 0.5 kg is free to rotate in a vertical plane about a fixed, smooth, horizontal axis through A. It is released from rest with AB horizontal.

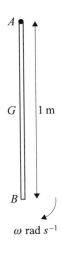

   (a) Calculate the potential energy lost by the rod in falling to the position where it is vertical with B below A.
   (b) Calculate the angular speed of the rod at this instant.

(a) The centre of mass G of the rod is at its mid-point.

So: P.E. lost $=$ mass $\times$ g $\times$ distance fallen by centre of mass
$$= 0.5 \times 9.8 \times 0.5 \, \text{J}$$
$$= 2.45 \, \text{J}$$

The potential energy lost is 2.45 J.

(b) Let the angular speed of the rod when AB is vertical be ω rad s^{-1}.

Use the standard result, $\tfrac{1}{3}ma^2$, for the moment of inertia of a uniform rod with mass m and length $2a$ about an axis through its mid-point, perpendicular to its length:

M.I. of rod about axis through its centre of mass G
$$= \tfrac{1}{3} \times 0.5 \times 0.5^2 \, \text{kg m}^2$$

Distance from G to end of rod $= 0.5 \, \text{m}$

So, by the parallel axis rule:

M.I. of rod about given axis through A
$$= (\tfrac{1}{3} \times 0.5^3 + 0.5 \times 0.5^2) \, \text{kg m}^2$$
$$= \tfrac{4}{3} \times 0.5^3 \, \text{kg m}^2$$
$$= \tfrac{4}{3} \times \tfrac{1}{2} \times \tfrac{1}{2} \times \tfrac{1}{2} \, \text{kg m}^2$$
$$= \tfrac{1}{6} \, \text{kg m}^2$$

So: K.E. of rod $= \tfrac{1}{2}I\omega^2 = \tfrac{1}{2} \times \tfrac{1}{6}\omega^2 \, \text{J}$

By the principle of conservation of mechanical energy:

$$\text{K.E. gained by rod} = \text{P.E. lost by rod}$$
$$\tfrac{1}{12}\omega^2 = 2.45$$
$$\omega^2 = 12 \times 2.45$$
$$\omega = 5.42$$

The angular speed of the rod is $5.42\,\text{rad s}^{-1}$.

Example 3

A pulley wheel has mass 2 kg and radius 0.25 m. One end of a rope is attached to a point on the rim of the wheel and the rope is wound several times around the rim. A brick of mass 0.5 kg attached to the other end of the rope hangs freely. The brick is released from rest. Assuming the axis of rotation of the wheel is horizontal, perpendicular to the wheel, and passes through the centre of the wheel, determine how far the brick must descend before it has acquired a speed of $2\,\text{m s}^{-1}$. State clearly any additional assumptions you make in order to model this situation.

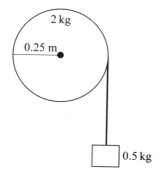

Assume that the axis is smooth and so there are no external forces acting.

Assume that the pulley wheel can be modelled as a uniform disc and the brick as a particle.

Assume that the rope is light and inextensible.

When the brick has a speed of $2\,\text{m s}^{-1}$, the (linear) speed of a point on the rim of the pulley wheel must be $2\,\text{m s}^{-1}$.

The angular speed ω and the linear speed v are related by the equation

$$v = r\omega$$

where r is the radius of the disc.

So:
$$2 = 0.25\omega$$

Hence the angular speed is $8\,\text{rad s}^{-1}$.

$$\text{M.I. of wheel} = \tfrac{1}{2}mr^2$$
$$= \tfrac{1}{2} \times 2 \times 0.25^2 \,\text{kg m}^2$$
$$= 0.25^2 \,\text{kg m}^2$$

So:
$$\text{K.E. gained by wheel} = \tfrac{1}{2}I\omega^2$$
$$= \tfrac{1}{2} \times 0.25^2 \times 8^2 \,\text{J}$$
$$= 2\,\text{J}$$

$$\text{K.E. gained by brick} = \tfrac{1}{2}mv^2$$
$$= \tfrac{1}{2} \times 0.5 \times 2^2 \, \text{J}$$
$$= 1 \, \text{J}$$

$$\text{P.E. lost by brick} = mgh = 0.5 \times 9.8h \, \text{J}$$

where h m is the distance the brick has fallen.

By the conservation of mechanical energy:

$$\text{P.E. lost} = \text{K.E. gained}$$

So:
$$0.5 \times 9.8h = 2 + 1$$

$$h = \frac{3}{0.5 \times 9.8} = 0.612$$

The brick must descend a distance 0.612 m.

Exercise 2A

1 A uniform circular hoop of mass 2 kg and radius 0.5 m is rotating in a horizontal plane about a smooth vertical axis through a point on its circumference. Calculate its kinetic energy when it is rotating at $4 \, \text{rad s}^{-1}$.

2 A uniform circular disc of mass 3 kg and radius 0.4 m has particles of mass 0.1 kg, 0.4 kg and 1 kg attached to points at distances 0.2 m, 0.2 m and 0.3 m respectively from the centre of the disc. The disc is rotating in a horizontal plane about a smooth vertical axis through its centre. Calculate the kinetic energy of the loaded disc when it is rotating at $3 \, \text{rad s}^{-1}$.

The disc is now brought to rest. Calculate the work done by the retarding force.

3 A uniform rod of length 1.2 m and mass 0.8 kg has particles of mass 0.2 kg and 0.5 kg attached, one at each end. The rod is rotating in a horizontal plane about a smooth vertical axis. Given that the rod is rotating with angular speed $5 \, \text{rad s}^{-1}$, calculate the kinetic energy of the rod:
(a) when the axis passes through the mid-point of the rod
(b) when the axis passes through the centre of mass of the loaded rod.

4 A uniform rod AB of length 1.5 m and mass 2 kg is smoothly pivoted at A. It is initially at rest with B vertically above A. It is slightly disturbed and rotates in a vertical plane.

(a) Calculate the potential energy lost by the rod when it reaches the horizontal position.

(b) Calculate the angular speed of the rod as it passes through the horizontal position.

(c) Calculate the angular speed of the rod when B is vertically below A.

5 A pulley wheel of mass 5 kg and radius 2 m has one end of a rope attached to a point of its rim and wound several times around its rim. A brick of mass 2 kg attached to the other end of the rope hangs freely 3 m above the ground. The brick is released from rest. Assuming that the pulley wheel can be modelled as a uniform disc which can rotate in a vertical plane about a smooth horizontal axis through its centre and the rope can be modelled as a light inextensible string, calculate the angular speed of the wheel when the brick hits the ground. State the model used for the brick in this calculation.

6 A uniform rod AB of mass m and length $4l$ is free to rotate in a vertical plane about a smooth horizontal axis through its mid-point. Particles of mass $3m$ and m are attached to ends A and B respectively.

(a) The rod is held with AB horizontal and then released from rest. Find, in terms of l and g, the angular speed of the rod when AB is vertical.

(b) If *instead* the rod is initially vertical with A below B and is then given an angular speed of $\sqrt{\left(\dfrac{g}{2l}\right)}$, calculate the angle between AB and the downward vertical when the rod first comes to rest.

7 A uniform disc of mass 1.5 kg and radius 1.5 m is free to rotate in a vertical plane about a smooth horizontal axis through its centre. A rope is attached to a point on the rim of the disc and wound around the disc. The disc is initially at rest. The free end of the rope is then pulled in a direction in the plane of the disc as shown in the diagram. Given that the tension in the rope is

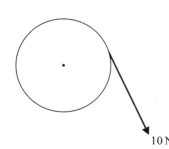

10 N

10 N, calculate the angle the disc has turned through when the angular speed is $3 \, \text{rad s}^{-1}$.

8   A uniform rod AB of mass m and length $2l$ has a particle of mass $2m$ attached to end B. The rod is free to rotate in a vertical plane about a smooth horizontal axis through the point C of the rod where $AC = \dfrac{l}{3}$. When the rod is hanging in equilibrium with B vertically below A it is given an angular speed of ω.

(a) Find the least possible value of ω if the rod is to perform complete revolutions.

(b) If ω is twice this minimum value, find the speed of the particle as it passes through its highest point.

(c) If ω is half this minimum value find the angle between BC and the downward vertical when the particle is at its highest point.

9   A uniform rod AB of mass m has a particle of mass m attached at B. The rod rotates in a vertical plane about a smooth horizontal axis through A. The greatest angular speed of the rod is $2\sqrt{\left(\dfrac{g}{l}\right)}$.

(a) Given that the rod just makes complete revolutions find the length of the rod.

(b) As end B passes through its lowest point a variable force is applied to the rod. The rod continues to rotate and B passes vertically above A with an angular speed of $\dfrac{3}{2}\sqrt{\left(\dfrac{g}{l}\right)}$.

Calculate the work done by the force in moving B from the lowest point to the highest point of its path.

10   A uniform wire in the form of a circle of radius a is free to rotate about a smooth horizontal axis through a point A of its circumference and perpendicular to its plane. It is released from rest with the diameter AB horizontal. Find its angular speed when AB is vertical.

11   A bucket of mass m is attached to the end of a light rope the other end of which is attached to the circumference of a wheel of mass M. The rope is wound several times around the wheel. The wheel can rotate freely about a smooth fixed horizontal axis through its centre. Assuming that the entire mass of the

wheel is concentrated in its rim, calculate the speed of the bucket when it has fallen a distance h from rest.

12 The figure shows an advertising sign in the form of a rectangular plate of sides $2a$ and $2b$. It is free to rotate about a smooth fixed horizontal axis which coincides with the side AB.

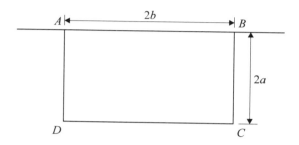

When the sign is hanging freely below the axis it is given an angular speed of $\left(\dfrac{kg}{a}\right)^{\frac{1}{2}}$. Determine the range of values of k for which the sign makes complete revolutions. State the mathematical model used for the sign in the calculation.

2.2 The equation of rotational motion

Consider a rigid body which is rotating about a fixed smooth axis which passes through the body. Think of the body as composed of particles $P_1, P_2, \ldots, P_n$, of masses $m_1, m_2, \ldots, m_n$, which are at distances $r_1, r_2, \ldots, r_n$ from the axis. The diagram shows a plane section of the body, perpendicular to the axis and containing the particle P_i. The axis of rotation passes through the point O of this section. When the body is rotating with angular speed $\dot{\theta}$ each line OP_i is also rotating with angular speed $\dot{\theta}$. The particle shown is therefore moving in a circle, centre on the axis, radius r_i, with angular speed $\dot{\theta}$. As was shown in Book M2, chapter 4, the acceleration of P_i has components $r_i\dot{\theta}^2$ along P_iO and $r_i\ddot{\theta}$ perpendicular to OP_i, respectively. Let the force acting on P_i have component N_i in the direction perpendicular to OP_i. Then applying Newton's second law to P_i in this direction gives:

$$N_i = m_i r_i \ddot{\theta}$$

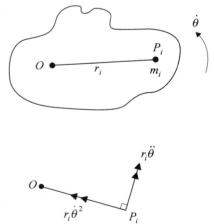

and multiplying by r_i:

$$N_i r_i = m_i r_i^2 \ddot{\theta}$$

As P_i is just one constituent particle of the rigid body, summing over all the particles $P_1, P_2, \ldots, P_n$ gives, for the whole body:

$$\sum_i N_i r_i = \sum_i m_i r_i^2 \ddot{\theta}$$

Since the body is rigid, that is, the particles cannot move relative to one another, $\ddot{\theta}$ is the same for all the particles. So:

$$\sum_i N_i r_i = \left(\sum_i m_i r_i^2 \right) \ddot{\theta}$$

And $\sum_i m_i r_i^2$ is just the moment of inertia, I, of the body about the axis through O, so:

$$\sum_i N_i r_i = I \ddot{\theta}$$

$\sum_i N_i r_i$ is the sum of the moments about the axis of rotation of the forces acting on each particle of the body (Book M1, chapter 6). It is the same as the moment about the axis of rotation of the resultant force acting on the body. This moment can be denoted by L, giving **the equation of rotational motion**:

■

$$L = I \ddot{\theta}$$

> where L **is the moment of the resultant force on a body about the axis of rotation**, I **is the moment of inertia of the body about the axis and** $\ddot{\theta}$ **is the angular acceleration of the body.**

Example 4

A pulley wheel has mass 1 kg and radius 0.25 m. A rope has one end attached to a point of the rim of the wheel and is wound several times around the rim. A brick of mass 0.5 kg attached to the other end of the rope hangs freely. The wheel is free to rotate in a vertical plane about a fixed, smooth, horizontal axis through the centre of the wheel. The brick is released from rest. By modelling the pulley wheel as a uniform disc, the brick as a particle and the rope as a light, inextensible string, calculate the tension in the rope and the acceleration of the brick.

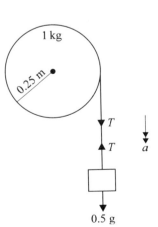

Let the tension be T N and the acceleration of the brick be $a\,\mathrm{m\,s^{-2}}$.

As in the motion of two connected particles, you must consider the motions of the disc and the brick separately.

For the brick, using the equation of motion, $F = ma$, gives:

$$0.5\,g - T = 0.5a \qquad (1)$$

For the pulley wheel, the linear acceleration of a point on the rim is $a\,\mathrm{m\,s^{-2}}$. Hence the angular acceleration, $\ddot{\theta}\,\mathrm{rad\,s^{-2}}$, of the wheel is given by:

$$r\ddot{\theta} = a$$

and since $r = 0.25\,\mathrm{m}$,

$$\ddot{\theta} = \frac{a}{0.25}$$

The moment of inertia of the wheel is $\frac{1}{2} \times 1 \times 0.25^2\,\mathrm{kg\,m^2}$. Using the equation of rotational motion, $L = I\ddot{\theta}$ gives:

$$T \times 0.25 = \tfrac{1}{2} \times 1 \times 0.25^2 \times \frac{a}{0.25}$$

So:
$$T = \tfrac{1}{2}a$$

Substituting for a in equation (1) gives:

$$0.5g - T = T$$
$$2T = 0.5 \times 9.8$$
$$T = 2.45$$

and so:
$$a = 2T = 2 \times 2.45 = 4.9$$

The tension is $2.45\,\mathrm{N}$ and the acceleration is $4.9\,\mathrm{m\,s^{-2}}$.

2.3 The force on the axis of rotation

To be able to calculate the force exerted by a rotating body on the axis of rotation we must first study the motion of the centre of mass of a system of particles. Consider a system of moving particles $P_1, P_2, \ldots, P_n$ of masses $m_1, m_2, \ldots, m_n$. Let the resultant force acting on P_i be $\mathbf{F}_i$ and let P_i have position vector $\mathbf{r}_i$ relative to some fixed origin O.

Applying Newton's second law to P_i gives:

$$\mathbf{F}_i = m_i \ddot{\mathbf{r}}_i$$

So for the whole system

$$\sum_i \mathbf{F}_i = \sum_i m_i \ddot{\mathbf{r}}_i \qquad (1)$$

Let $\sum_i m_i = M$ and let the centre of mass have position vector $\mathbf{r}_G$

given by

$$\sum_i m_i \mathbf{r}_i = M \mathbf{r}_G \qquad (2)$$

Differentiating equation (2) twice with respect to time gives:

$$\sum_i m_i \ddot{\mathbf{r}}_i = M \ddot{\mathbf{r}}_G \qquad (3)$$

as m_i, M are constants.

Eliminating $\sum_i m_i \ddot{\mathbf{r}}_i$ from equations (1) and (3) gives:

$$\sum_i \mathbf{F}_i = M \ddot{\mathbf{r}}_G$$

But $\sum_i \mathbf{F}_i$ is the resultant of all the forces acting on the system, so:

- **The centre of mass of a system of particles has the same acceleration as a particle of mass equal to the total mass of the system situated at the centre of mass under the action of a force equal to the resultant of all the forces acting on the system.**

You can treat a rigid body as if it were a system of particles and so this principle applies. Hence:

- **For a rigid body which is rotating about a fixed smooth axis, the force exerted by the axis on the body can be calculated by considering the motion of a particle of the same mass as the body placed at the centre of mass of the body under the action of the same forces as those acting on the body.**

Suppose a body of mass m is rotating about a smooth, fixed, horizontal axis and that its centre of mass G is a distance r from the axis of rotation. The diagram shows the vertical plane through the centre of mass with the axis of rotation passing through O.

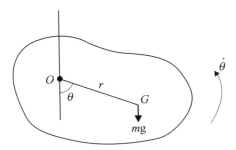

Let the angular speed of the body be $\dot{\theta}$ and consider a particle of mass m placed at G. The particle is moving in a vertical circle, radius r, with angular speed $\dot{\theta}$. The angle between OG and the downward vertical is θ.

The particle's acceleration has components $r\dot{\theta}^2$ and $r\ddot{\theta}$ parallel to GO and perpendicular to OG respectively:

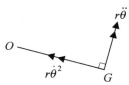

Let the force *from* the axis have components X and Y parallel to GO and perpendicular to OG. The mass of the body is m and the forces acting are X, Y and mg. The equation of motion parallel to GO gives:

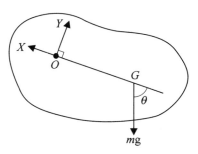

$$X - mg\cos\theta = mr\dot{\theta}^2$$

The equation of motion perpendicular to OG gives:

$$Y - mg\sin\theta = mr\ddot{\theta}$$

The value of $r\dot{\theta}^2$ can be found for any position of the body by using the principle of conservation of mechanical energy. The value of $r\ddot{\theta}$ can be found from the equation of rotational motion. Alternatively, differentiating $r\dot{\theta}^2$ with respect to θ gives:

$$\frac{\mathrm{d}}{\mathrm{d}\theta}(r\dot{\theta}^2) = 2r\dot{\theta}\,\frac{\mathrm{d}\dot{\theta}}{\mathrm{d}\theta}$$

by the chain rule (Book P2, chapter 8)

$$= 2r\dot{\theta}\,\frac{\mathrm{d}\dot{\theta}}{\mathrm{d}t}\cdot\frac{\mathrm{d}t}{\mathrm{d}\theta}$$

and as $\dot{\theta} = \dfrac{\mathrm{d}\theta}{\mathrm{d}t}$ and $\dfrac{\mathrm{d}\dot{\theta}}{\mathrm{d}t} = \dfrac{\mathrm{d}^2\theta}{\mathrm{d}t^2} = \ddot{\theta}$ this gives

$$\frac{\mathrm{d}}{\mathrm{d}\theta}(r\dot{\theta}^2) = 2r\ddot{\theta}$$

Hence the value of $\ddot{\theta}$ can be found by differentiating with respect to θ an expression for $r\dot{\theta}^2$ in terms of θ. Thus you can calculate the components X and Y of the force exerted *by the axis on the body*. Usually you are asked for the force exerted *on the axis*, and so you must use Newton's third law as a final step.

Example 5

A uniform circular disc, centre C, of mass m and radius r can rotate in a vertical plane about a smooth horizontal axis through a point A on its rim. Initially, the disc is held at rest with AC horizontal. It is then released. Find the components of the force on the axis when AC makes an angle θ with the downward vertical.

Calculate the magnitude of the force on the axis (a) when AC is vertical and (b) when $\theta = \dfrac{\pi}{3}$.

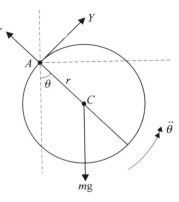

The angular acceleration of the disc is $\ddot{\theta}$.

Let the force from the axis of rotation have components X and Y along and perpendicular to CA as shown.

Consider the motion of a particle of mass m, placed at the centre of mass C of the disc, when the resultant force acting on the particle is the same as the resultant force acting on the disc. This particle will be moving in a vertical circle, centre A, radius r. It will therefore have accelerations $r\ddot{\theta}$ perpendicular to AC and $r\dot{\theta}^2$ along CA:

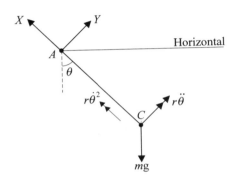

Applying Newton's second law parallel to CA gives:

$$X - mg\cos\theta = mr\dot{\theta}^2 \qquad (1)$$

and Newton's second law perpendicular to CA gives:

$$Y - mg\sin\theta = mr\ddot{\theta} \qquad (2)$$

You can find $r\dot{\theta}^2$ and $r\ddot{\theta}$ by considering the rotational motion of the disc.

M.I. of disc about axis through centre $C = \frac{1}{2}mr^2$

M.I. of disc about axis through $A = \frac{1}{2}mr^2 + mr^2 = \frac{3}{2}mr^2$

By the principle of conservation of mechanical energy:

K.E. gained by disc = P.E. lost by disc

P.E. lost $= mgr\cos\theta$

K.E. gained $= \frac{1}{2}I\dot{\theta}^2 = \frac{1}{2} \times \frac{3}{2}mr^2\dot{\theta}^2$

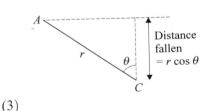

So:
$$\frac{3}{4}mr^2\dot{\theta}^2 = mgr\cos\theta$$
$$r\dot{\theta}^2 = \frac{4}{3}g\cos\theta \qquad (3)$$

Applying the equation of rotational motion:

$$\text{moment of resultant force about axis} = I\ddot{\theta}$$

$$mgr \sin \theta = -\tfrac{3}{2}mr^2\ddot{\theta}$$

So:
$$r\ddot{\theta} = -\tfrac{2}{3}g \sin \theta$$

Alternatively, differentiating equation (3) with respect to θ gives:

$$2r\ddot{\theta} = -\tfrac{4}{3}g \sin \theta$$

and so:
$$r\ddot{\theta} = -\tfrac{2}{3}g \sin \theta$$

Substituting $r\dot{\theta}^2 = \tfrac{4}{3}g \cos \theta$ and $r\ddot{\theta} = -\tfrac{2}{3}g \sin \theta$ in equations (1) and (2) gives:

$$X - mg \cos \theta = \tfrac{4}{3}mg \cos \theta$$
$$Y - mg \sin \theta = -\tfrac{2}{3}mg \sin \theta$$

And so:
$$X = \tfrac{7}{3}mg \cos \theta, \quad Y = \tfrac{1}{3}mg \sin \theta$$

But X and Y are the components of the force exerted *by* the axis *on* the disc. By Newton's third law, the force exerted *on* the axis *by* the disc has components of equal magnitude but opposite direction.

So the force on the axis has components:

$$\tfrac{7}{3}mg \cos \theta \text{ along } AC$$

and

$$\tfrac{1}{3}mg \sin \theta \text{ perpendicular to } AC$$

(in the direction of decreasing θ).

(a) When AC is vertical, $\theta = 0$. So the magnitude of the force on the axis is $\tfrac{7}{3}mg$. Note that the component of the force perpendicular to AC is zero when AC is vertical.

(b) When $\theta = \tfrac{\pi}{3}$ the components are:

$$\tfrac{7}{3}mg \times \tfrac{1}{2} = \frac{7mg}{6} \text{ along } AC$$

and
$$\tfrac{1}{3}mg \times \frac{\sqrt{3}}{2} = \frac{mg\sqrt{3}}{6} \text{ perpendicular to } AC.$$

So the resultant force has magnitude

$$\sqrt{\left\{\frac{49m^2g^2}{36} + m^2g^2 \times \frac{3}{36}\right\}} = mg\sqrt{\left(\frac{52}{36}\right)} = \frac{mg\sqrt{13}}{3}$$

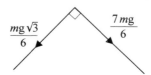

Exercise 2B

1 A uniform rod of length $2a$ and mass m is free to rotate in a horizontal plane about a fixed vertical axis through one end. A horizontal force of constant magnitude $5mg$ is applied to its free end at right angles to the rod. Find the magnitude of the resulting angular acceleration.

2 A uniform circular disc of radius $0.2\,m$ and mass $0.5\,kg$ is free to rotate in a horizontal plane about a smooth, fixed, vertical axis through its centre. A horizontal force of constant magnitude is applied at a point on the rim of the disc in the direction of a tangent to the disc. The disc rotates with angular acceleration $5\,rad\,s^{-2}$. Calculate the magnitude of the force.

3 A pulley wheel of mass $2\,kg$ has one end of a rope attached to a point of its rim and the rope is wound several times around the rim. The wheel is free to rotate about a fixed, smooth, horizontal axis through its centre and perpendicular to the wheel. A brick hangs freely, attached to the other end of the rope. The brick is released from rest and falls $10\,m$ in the first two seconds after its release. Assuming that the pulley can be modelled as a uniform circular disc and the brick as a particle, calculate the tension in the rope and the mass of the brick.

4 A uniform rod AB of mass $2m$ and length $3a$ is free to rotate in a vertical plane about a fixed, smooth, horizontal axis through end A of the rod. A particle of mass m is attached to end B. The rod is released from rest with AB horizontal. Find (a) the initial angular acceleration of the system (b) the angular acceleration when the rod has turned through an angle θ.

5 A uniform solid cylinder of radius $0.5\,m$ and mass $0.5\,kg$ can rotate freely about a smooth, fixed, horizontal axis which coincides with the axis of the cylinder. A light string passes over the cylinder in a vertical plane perpendicular to the axis of rotation. Particles of masses $0.25\,kg$ and $0.5\,kg$ are attached one to each end of the string and the system is released from rest. Assuming that the string does not slip on the cylinder and that neither particle has reached the cylinder, calculate the tensions

in the two parts of the string and the angular acceleration of the cylinder.

6 A uniform rod AB of mass m and length $2a$ is free to rotate in a vertical plane about a fixed, smooth, horizontal axis through the point C of the rod where $AC = \frac{1}{2}a$. The rod is released from rest with AB horizontal. Calculate the magnitude of the force exerted on the axis (a) when AB is vertical with B below A (b) when AB makes an angle of $60°$ with the downward vertical.

7 A uniform rod AB of mass m and length $8a$ is free to rotate in a vertical plane about a smooth, fixed, horizontal axis through the point C of the rod where $AC = 2a$. The rod is initially at rest with A vertically below C but is then slightly disturbed and begins to rotate. Find (a) the angular speed when the rod has turned through an angle θ (b) the magnitude of the force on the axis when the rod is vertical with A vertically above C.

8 A uniform square lamina $ABCD$ of mass m and side $2a$ is free to rotate about a smooth, horizontal axis through A. The axis is perpendicular to the plane of the lamina. The lamina is in equilibrium with C vertically below A when it is given an angular speed $2\sqrt{\left(\frac{g}{a}\right)}$. Show that the lamina will perform complete revolutions and find the horizontal and vertical components of the reaction at A (a) when AC is horizontal (b) when C is vertically above A.

9 A uniform circular disc, centre O, of mass $2m$ and radius r has a particle of mass m attached to a point A of its surface where $OA = \frac{1}{2}r$. The disc is free to rotate about a fixed, smooth, horizontal axis through O, perpendicular to the plane of the disc. The disc is held at rest with A vertically above O. The disc is slightly disturbed from its position of rest. Find the horizontal and vertical components of the force on the axis (a) when OA is horizontal (b) when A is vertically below O.

2.4 Angular momentum

As before, consider a rigid body rotating about a fixed axis. Consider the body to be composed of particles $P_1, P_2, \ldots, P_n$ of masses $m_1, m_2, \ldots, m_n$, respectively. Assume that the rigid body is rotating about the axis with angular speed $\dot{\theta}$.

The diagram shows a plane section of the body, perpendicular to the axis and containing the particle P_i. The axis of rotation passes through the point O of this section and P_i is at a distance r_i from O.

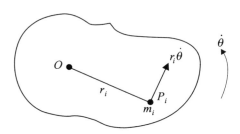

The particle P_i is moving in a circle of radius r_i and so has linear speed $r_i\dot{\theta}$ as shown. The linear momentum of P_i is therefore $m_i r_i \dot{\theta}$. As momentum is a vector, it has a moment about the axis through O which is calculated in the same manner as is the moment of a force. So for the particle P_i, the moment of the momentum about the axis through O is given by

$$\text{moment of momentum} = (m_i r_i \dot{\theta}) r_i$$
$$= m_i r_i^2 \dot{\theta}$$

Hence for the whole body,

$$\text{moment of momentum about axis through } O = \sum_i m_i r_i^2 \dot{\theta}$$
$$= \dot{\theta} \sum_i m_i r_i^2 = I\dot{\theta}$$

The moment of momentum is often called the **angular momentum** of the body.

When the mass is measured in kilograms, lengths in metres and angular speed in rad s^{-1}, the angular momentum is measured in $\text{kg m}^2 \text{s}^{-1}$.

Example 6
A uniform rod AB of mass 0.5 kg and length 1.2 m has a particle of mass 1.5 kg attached to end B. The rod can rotate in a horizontal plane about a smooth vertical axis through A. Calculate the angular momentum of the rod and particle when the rod is rotating with angular speed 5 rad s^{-1}.

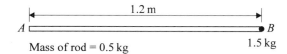

M.I. of rod about axis through mid-point perpendicular to rod
$= \frac{1}{3} \times 0.5 \times 0.6^2 \, \text{kg m}^2 = 0.06 \, \text{kg m}^2$.

M.I. of rod about axis through A perpendicular to rod
$= (0.06 + 0.5 \times 0.6^2) \, \text{kg m}^2 = 0.24 \, \text{kg m}^2$ (parallel axis theorem).

M.I. of particle about axis through A perpendicular to rod
$= 1.5 \times 1.2^2 \, \text{kg m}^2 = 2.16 \, \text{kg m}^2$.

M.I. of rod and particle about axis through A perpendicular to rod
$= (0.24 + 2.16) \, \text{kg m}^2 = 2.4 \, \text{kg m}^2$.

$$\text{Angular speed} = 5 \, \text{rad s}^{-1}$$

So
$$\begin{aligned}
\text{angular momentum} &= I\dot{\theta} \\
&= 2.4 \times 5 \, \text{kg m}^2 \, \text{s}^{-1} \\
&= 12 \, \text{kg m}^2 \, \text{s}^{-1}
\end{aligned}$$

2.5 Conservation of angular momentum

When any two bodies A and B collide, by Newton's third law they exert equal but opposite impulses on each other. If the motion of at least one of the bodies is rotational then the moments of these impulses about the axis of rotation must also be equal but opposite.

Suppose A is rotating and let the moment of the impulse on A from B be M. Then the moment of the impulse on B is $-M$. Provided there are no external forces which have a moment about the axis of rotation, the gain of angular momentum of A and B is zero. This is the **principle of conservation of angular momentum**.

■ **Provided there are no external forces on a system with a moment about the axis of rotation, the total angular momentum of the system is constant.**

Example 7

A uniform rod AB of length 1.6 m and mass 3 kg is at rest on a smooth, horizontal table. AB is free to rotate on the table about a smooth, vertical axis through end A. A particle P of mass 0.6 kg is moving at $2 \, \text{m s}^{-1}$ on the table at right angles to AB and strikes the rod at C where $AC = 0.9$ m. P adheres to the rod. Calculate the angular speed with which the rod begins to rotate.

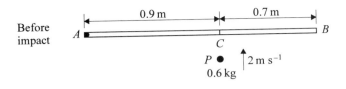

Let the rod begin to rotate with angular speed $\omega \, \text{rad s}^{-1}$.

M.I. of rod about axis through centre perpendicular to rod

$$= \tfrac{1}{3}ma^2 = \tfrac{1}{3} \times 3 \times \left(\frac{1.6}{2}\right)^2 \text{kg m}^2 = 0.64 \, \text{kg m}^2$$

M.I. of rod about axis through A perpendicular to rod

$$= (0.64 + 3 \times 0.8^2) \, \text{kg m}^2 = 2.56 \, \text{kg m}^2$$

Initial angular momentum of rod $= 0 \, \text{kg m}^2\text{s}^{-1}$

Final angular momentum of rod about axis through A perpendicular to rod $= I\omega = 2.56\omega \, \text{kg m}^2 \, \text{s}^{-1}$

Just before hitting the rod, P is moving at right angles to AB with a speed of $2 \, \text{m s}^{-1}$ at a distance $0.9 \, \text{m}$ from A.

So: linear momentum of $P = 0.6 \times 2 \, \text{N s} = 1.2 \, \text{N s}$

Initial moment of momentum of P about vertical axis through A

$$= 1.2 \times 0.9 \, \text{kg m}^2 \, \text{s}^{-1}$$
$$= 1.08 \, \text{kg m}^2 \, \text{s}^{-1}$$

Just after the impact P is moving in a circle, radius $0.9 \, \text{m}$, centre A, with a linear speed of $0.9\omega \, \text{m s}^{-1}$.

So final moment of momentum of P about vertical axis through A

$$= mvr = 0.6 \times 0.9\omega \times 0.9 \, \text{kg m}^2 \, \text{s}^{-1}$$
$$= 0.486\omega \, \text{kg m}^2 \, \text{s}^{-1}$$

By the principle of conservation of angular momentum:

$$0 + 1.08 = 2.56\omega + 0.486\omega$$

$$\omega = \frac{1.08}{3.046} = 0.355$$

The rod begins to rotate with an angular speed of $0.355 \, \text{rad s}^{-1}$.

2.6 Effect of an impulse on a rigid body which is free to rotate about a fixed axis

Consider a rigid body which is free to rotate about a fixed axis. The equation of rotational motion states:

$$L = I\ddot{\theta}$$

where $\ddot{\theta}$ is the angular acceleration of the body and L and I are the moment of the resultant force on the body and the moment of inertia of the body, respectively, about the axis of rotation.

Integrating with respect to time gives:

$$\int_{t_1}^{t_2} L \, dt = \int_{\omega_1}^{\omega_2} I\ddot{\theta} \, dt$$

where ω_1, ω_2 are the angular speeds at times t_1 and t_2 respectively.

$$\int_{t_1}^{t_2} L \, dt = \left[I\dot{\theta} \right]_{\omega_1}^{\omega_2}$$

$$\int_{t_1}^{t_2} L \, dt = I\omega_2 - I\omega_1 \qquad (1)$$

$\int_{t_1}^{t_2} L \, dt$ is the **impulsive moment** of the resultant force about the axis and $(I\omega_2 - I\omega_1)$ is the gain of angular momentum. So equation (1) can be expressed in the form:

■ **impulsive moment of the force = gain of angular momentum**

Sometimes a rigid body is rotating under the action of a force of constant magnitude F acting at a constant distance r from the axis in a plane perpendicular to the axis. A cylinder rotating about its axis with a string wound around its circumference which is being pulled with a constant tension would be an example of this.

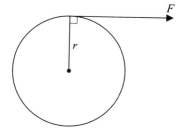

In this case, $\qquad L = F \times r$

So: $\qquad \int_{t_1}^{t_2} L \, dt = \int_{t_1}^{t_2} F \times r \, dt = Fr(t_2 - t_1) = F(t_2 - t_1)r$

and hence:

impulsive moment of force = moment of force
$\qquad\qquad\qquad\qquad\qquad \times$ time for which force acts

or: $\qquad$ impulsive moment = impulse $\times$ distance from axis

Impulsive moment is measured in N m s.

As impulsive moment equals change of angular momentum it follows that angular momentum also has units $\mathrm{N\,m\,s}$. In other words, $\mathrm{kg\,m^2\,s^{-1}}$ and $\mathrm{N\,m\,s}$ are equivalent units.

Example 8

A uniform rod $A\dot{B}$ of mass $2\,\mathrm{kg}$ and length $0.9\,\mathrm{m}$ rests on a smooth, horizontal table and is free to rotate about a vertical axis through the end A. The rod receives a blow from a hammer at its free end in a direction perpendicular to the rod and begins to rotate at $10\,\mathrm{rad\,s^{-1}}$. Calculate the impulse of the blow.

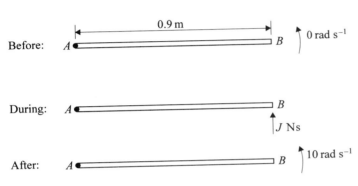

Let the impulse be $J\,\mathrm{N\,s}$.

Moment of impulse about $A = 0.9J\,\mathrm{N\,m\,s}$

M.I. of rod about axis through centre perpendicular to rod

$$= \tfrac{1}{3}ma^2 = \tfrac{1}{3} \times 2 \times 0.45^2\,\mathrm{kg\,m^2} = 0.135\,\mathrm{kg\,m^2}$$

M.I. of rod about axis through A perpendicular to rod

$$= (0.135 + 2 \times 0.45^2)\,\mathrm{kg\,m^2}$$
$$= 0.54\,\mathrm{kg\,m^2}$$

Initial angular momentum of rod $= 0\,\mathrm{N\,m\,s}$

Final angular momentum of rod $= I\omega$
$$= 0.54 \times 10\,\mathrm{N\,m\,s}$$
$$= 5.4\,\mathrm{N\,m\,s}$$

But: moment of impulse $=$ gain of angular momentum

So: $$0.9J = 5.4$$

and: $$J = \frac{5.4}{0.9} = 6$$

The impulse is $6\,\mathrm{N\,s}$.

Example 9

A pulley of mass m and radius r is free to rotate in a vertical plane about a smooth, horizontal axis through its centre O. One end of a light inextensible string is attached to a point on the rim of the pulley. The string is wrapped several times around the pulley; a length of $5r$ remains free. A particle P of mass $2m$ is attached to the free end of the string. P is held close to the rim of the pulley, with OP horizontal, and is then released from rest.

(a) State a suitable model for the pulley.
(b) Find, in terms of r and g, the angular speed of the pulley immediately after the string becomes taut.

(a) The pulley can be modelled as a uniform disc.

(b)

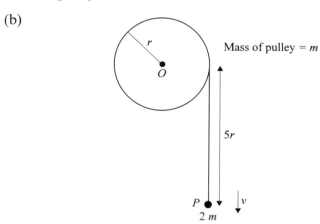

Mass of pulley $= m$

Let the speed of P immediately before the string becomes taut be v and the angular speed of the disc immediately after the string becomes taut be ω. P has then fallen a distance $5r$ from rest.

Using $v^2 = u^2 + 2as$ with $u = 0$, $a = $ g, and $s = 5r$ gives:

$$v^2 = 2 \times \text{g} \times 5r$$
$$v^2 = 10gr$$
$$v = \sqrt{(10gr)}$$

So the linear momentum of P just before the jerk as the string becomes taut is

$$2mv = 2m\sqrt{(10gr)}$$

Initial moment of momentum of $P = 2m\sqrt{(10gr)} \times r$
$$= 2mr\sqrt{(10gr)}$$

Final linear momentum of $P = 2mr\omega$

$\therefore$ Final moment of momentum of $P = (2mr\omega)r = 2mr^2\omega$

M.I. of disc about axis through its centre $= \frac{1}{2}mr^2$

Initial angular momentum of disc $= 0$

Final angular momentum of disc $= I\omega = \frac{1}{2}mr^2\omega$

By the principle of conservation of angular momentum:

$$0 + 2mr\sqrt{(10gr)} = \frac{1}{2}mr^2\omega + 2mr^2\omega$$
$$2\sqrt{(10gr)} = \frac{5}{2}r\omega$$

$$\omega = \frac{4}{5}\sqrt{\left(\frac{10g}{r}\right)}$$

The angular speed of the pulley is $\frac{4}{5}\sqrt{\left(\frac{10g}{r}\right)}$.

Exercise 2C

1 A uniform disc of mass 1.5 kg and radius 2 m is rotating at a constant angular speed of $5\,\text{rad}\,\text{s}^{-1}$ about a perpendicular axis through its centre. Calculate the angular momentum of the disc.

2 A uniform square lamina of mass 2 kg and side 0.5 m is free to rotate about an axis which coincides with one of its sides. Calculate the loss of angular momentum when the angular speed of the lamina is reduced from $4\,\text{rad}\,\text{s}^{-1}$ to $1\,\text{rad}\,\text{s}^{-1}$.

3 A uniform rod AB of length $4a$ and mass m is free to rotate in a vertical plane about a smooth, fixed, horizontal axis through the point C of the rod where $AC = a$. The rod is released from rest with AB horizontal. When the rod first becomes vertical, end B strikes a stationary particle of mass m which adheres to the rod. Find, in terms of g and a, the angular speed of the rod after the impact and calculate the angle between the rod and the downward vertical when the rod comes to instantaneous rest.

4 A rectangular sign is hanging outside a shop. The sign has mass 2 kg and measures 1 m by 2 m. It is free to swing about a smooth, fixed, horizontal axis which coincides with a long side of the rectangle. The sign is initially hanging at rest when it

receives an impulse at its centre of mass in a direction perpendicular to its plane. The sign first comes to rest in a horizontal position. By assuming that the sign can be modelled as a uniform rectangular lamina, calculate the initial angular speed of the sign and the magnitude of the impulse.

5 A uniform rod AB of length $2a$ and mass m is free to rotate in a vertical plane about a fixed, smooth, horizontal axis through A. The rod is initially at rest with B vertically below A. The end B receives a horizontal impulse of magnitude J in a direction perpendicular to the axis of rotation. Find, in terms of m, g and a, the least value of J if the rod is to rotate in complete circles. Given that the magnitude of J is one half of this value, find the angle the rod turns through before first coming to instantaneous rest.

6 A uniform rod AB of mass 0.2 kg and length 0.8 m is free to rotate in a vertical plane about a fixed, smooth, horizontal axis through its centre. It is initially at rest in a horizontal position. A particle of mass 0.15 kg falls vertically onto the rod, and sticks to the rod at the point C where $AC = 0.1$ m. The rod subsequently makes complete revolutions. Calculate the minimum height above the rod from which the particle must have fallen.

7 A uniform solid cylindrical drum of mass 1.5 kg and radius 0.5 m is free to rotate about a fixed, smooth, horizontal axis which coincides with the axis of the cylinder. The axis is at a height of 2 m above a horizontal table and a light string AB of length 4 m has one end attached to the highest point of the cylinder. A block of mass 0.3 kg is attached to end B of the string and rests on the table as shown in the diagram. The drum begins to rotate at a constant angular speed of 4 rad s^{-1} in a clockwise direction. Calculate the angular speed of the drum immediately after the block is jerked into motion.

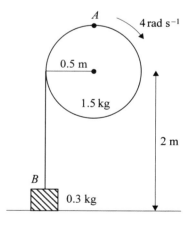

8 A uniform rod AB of mass m and length $6a$ is free to rotate about a fixed, smooth, vertical axis through the point C of AB, where $AC = 2a$. AB is at rest on a smooth, horizontal table when it is struck by a particle of mass $2m$ moving on the table in a direction perpendicular to the rod with speed u. The particle

adheres to the rod at D, where $DB = x$. Given that the speed of the particle is halved by the impact, find x.

9 A uniform rod AB of mass m and length $2a$ is free to rotate about a fixed, smooth, vertical axis through A. AB is at rest on a smooth, horizontal table. A particle P of mass $6m$ moving in a direction perpendicular to the rod with speed u hits the rod at C where $AC = \dfrac{3a}{4}$. P is brought to rest by the impact. Find the angular speed of the rod after the impact.

10 A uniform square lamina of mass m and side l is free to rotate about a fixed, smooth, horizontal axis which coincides with a side of the lamina. The lamina is hanging in equilibrium when it is hit at its centre of mass by a particle of mass $3m$ moving with speed v in a direction perpendicular to the plane of the lamina. The particle adheres to the lamina. Find, in terms of v and a, the angular speed of the lamina immediately after the impact. Hence show that the lamina will perform complete revolutions if

$$v^2 > \tfrac{104}{27}lg$$

11 Four rods, each of mass $3m$ and length $2l$, are joined together to form a square framework $ABCD$. The framework is free to rotate in its own plane about a smooth, fixed, horizontal axis through A perpendicular to the plane of the framework. The framework is hanging in equilibrium with C vertically below A when a horizontal impulse in the plane of the framework is applied at the mid-point of AB. The framework first comes to rest when AC makes an angle $\frac{\pi}{4}$ with the upward vertical. Find the magnitude of the impulse.
If instead the impulse were applied at the mid-point of BC, determine whether the framework would perform complete revolutions.

2.7 The compound pendulum

In Book M2, chapter 2, we considered the motion of a simple pendulum. This model consisted of a body that is making small oscillations, attached to one end of an inelastic string or rod whose other end was fixed. The model was valid provided the body had a large mass compared with that of the string or rod. This meant that the body could be modelled as a particle and the string or rod modelled as a light string. Now that we have studied the rotational motion of rigid bodies we can consider a more refined model – the compound pendulum.

Consider a rigid body which can rotate about a smooth, fixed, horizontal axis and is initially hanging in equilibrium. If it is slightly displaced, it will swing like a pendulum. Such a swinging body is called a **compound pendulum**. The diagram shows the vertical plane through the centre of mass, G, of the body. The axis passes through point O of this plane.

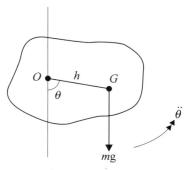

Let the body have mass m and let $OG = h$. When OG makes an angle θ with the downward vertical the angular acceleration of the body is $\ddot{\theta}$ as shown. Let the moment of inertia of the body about the given axis be I.

The moment of the weight of the body about the axis is $mgh \sin \theta \,\circlearrowright$. As this is the only force with a non-zero moment about the axis, the equation of rotational motion gives:

$$\text{moment of resultant force} = I\ddot{\theta} \,\circlearrowright$$

So

$$mgh \sin \theta = -I\ddot{\theta} \,\circlearrowright$$

For small oscillations, as with the simple pendulum, $\sin \theta \approx \theta$ and so:

$$\ddot{\theta} = \frac{-mgh\theta}{I} \qquad (1)$$

You should remember that an oscillation represented by the simple harmonic equation $\ddot{x} = -\omega^2 x$ has a period of $\dfrac{2\pi}{\omega}$ (Book M2, section 2.4). Comparing this with equation (1), ω is equivalent to $\sqrt{\left(\dfrac{mgh}{I}\right)}$.

So we have, approximately, an oscillation of period $2\pi\sqrt{\left(\dfrac{I}{mgh}\right)}$.

For a rigid body of mass m with radius of gyration k about a parallel axis through its centre of mass, G, the moment of inertia about a horizontal axis through G is mk^2. Hence, by the parallel axis rule, the moment of inertia I about the horizontal axis through O is given by:

$$I = mk^2 + mh^2 = m(k^2 + h^2)$$

The period of small oscillations about the axis through O for this body is now given by:

$$T = 2\pi \sqrt{\left(\frac{I}{mgh}\right)}$$

$$= 2\pi \sqrt{\left[\frac{m(k^2 + h^2)}{mgh}\right]}$$

- **So:**
$$T = 2\pi \sqrt{\left[\frac{k^2 + h^2}{gh}\right]}$$

Where h is the distance of the centre of mass, G, from the axis and k is the radius of gyration of the body about a parallel axis through G.

Example 10

A uniform rod AB of length $2a$ can swing in a vertical plane about a smooth, horizontal axis through point C of the rod where $AC = \dfrac{a}{2}$. Calculate the period of small oscillations of the rod about its equilibrium position.

Let the rod have mass m.

M.I. of rod about axis through centre, perpendicular to rod

$$= \tfrac{1}{3} ma^2$$

Radius of gyration, k, about same axis is given by

$$k^2 = \tfrac{1}{3} a^2$$

Period of small oscillations $= 2\pi \sqrt{\left[\dfrac{k^2 + h^2}{gh}\right]}$

$$= 2\pi \sqrt{\left[\frac{\frac{1}{3} a^2 + \frac{a^2}{4}}{g \frac{a}{2}}\right]}$$

$$= 2\pi \sqrt{\left[\frac{\frac{7a^2}{12}}{\frac{ga}{2}}\right]}$$

$$= 2\pi \sqrt{\left[\frac{7a}{6g}\right]}$$

Example 11

A thin uniform rod AB, of mass m and length $2a$, is free to rotate in a vertical plane about a fixed, smooth, horizontal axis through A. A uniform circular disc, of mass $3m$ and radius $\dfrac{a}{3}$, is clamped to the rod with its centre O on the rod so that it lies in the plane of rotation. If $OA = x$ show that the moment of inertia of the system about the axis is

$$\frac{3m}{2}(a^2 + 2x^2)$$

The system is initially hanging in equilibrium with B vertically below A. It is then slightly displaced and oscillates freely under gravity. Find the period of small oscillations and show that this is least when

$$x = \frac{a}{6}(\sqrt{22} - 2)$$

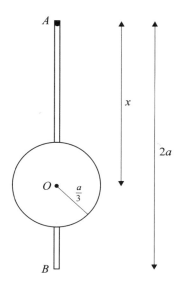

M.I. of rod about horizontal axis through mid-point

$$= \tfrac{1}{3}ma^2$$

M.I. of rod about horizontal axis through A

$$= \tfrac{1}{3}ma^2 + ma^2 = \tfrac{4}{3}ma^2$$

M.I. of disc about perpendicular axis through O

$$= \tfrac{1}{2} \times 3m \times \left(\frac{a}{3}\right)^2 = \frac{ma^2}{6}$$

M.I. of disc about parallel axis through A

$$= \frac{ma^2}{6} + 3mx^2$$

So M.I. of system about the given axis through A

$$= \frac{4ma^2}{3} + \frac{ma^2}{6} + 3mx^2$$

$$= \frac{9ma^2}{6} + 3mx^2$$

$$= \frac{3m}{2}(a^2 + 2x^2)$$

As the moment of inertia of the system about the given axis is now known, use the formula

$$T = 2\pi\sqrt{\left(\frac{I}{Mgh}\right)}$$

to find the period of small oscillations.

h is the distance of the centre of mass from the axis. So you must find the position of the centre of mass.

	Rod	Disc	Composite body
Mass	m	$3m$	$4m$
Distance of centre of mass from A	a	x	h

Taking moments about the axis of rotation gives:

$$ma + 3mx = 4mh$$

So:
$$h = \frac{a + 3x}{4}$$

Hence:
$$T = 2\pi\sqrt{\left(\frac{I}{Mgh}\right)}$$

where $I = \frac{3m}{2}(a^2 + 2x^2)$, $M = 4m$ and $h = \frac{a + 3x}{4}$.

So:
$$T = 2\pi\sqrt{\left[\frac{3m(a^2 + 2x^2) \times 4}{2 \times 4mg(a + 3x)}\right]}$$

$$= 2\pi\sqrt{\left[\frac{3(a^2 + 2x^2)}{2(a + 3x)g}\right]}$$

The period will be least when $\dfrac{(a^2 + 2x^2)}{(a + 3x)}$ is least.

Let $f(x) = \dfrac{(a^2 + 2x^2)}{(a + 3x)}$.

Then $f(x)$ is least when $\dfrac{df(x)}{dx} = 0$.

$$\frac{df(x)}{dx} = \frac{4x(a + 3x) - (a^2 + 2x^2) \times 3}{(a + 3x)^2}$$

$\dfrac{df(x)}{dx} = 0$ when

$$4x(a + 3x) - (a^2 + 2x^2) \times 3 = 0$$
$$4ax + 12x^2 - 3a^2 - 6x^2 = 0$$
$$6x^2 + 4ax - 3a^2 = 0$$

So:
$$x = \frac{-4a \pm \sqrt{(16a^2 + 72a^2)}}{12}$$
$$= \frac{-4a \pm \sqrt{(88a^2)}}{12}$$
$$= \frac{-4a \pm 2a\sqrt{22}}{12}$$
$$= \frac{-2a \pm a\sqrt{22}}{6}$$

As x must be positive,

$$x = \frac{-2a + a\sqrt{22}}{6}$$
$$= \frac{a}{6}(\sqrt{22} - 2)$$

The period of small oscillations is least when $x = \dfrac{a}{6}(\sqrt{22} - 2)$.

The equivalent simple pendulum

The simple pendulum which has the same period as a given compound pendulum is called the **equivalent simple pendulum**.

The length of the equivalent simple pendulum can be found by recalling that the period of a simple pendulum of length l is $2\pi\sqrt{\left(\dfrac{l}{g}\right)}$ (Book M2, chapter 2). From above, the period of the compound pendulum is $2\pi\sqrt{\left(\dfrac{I}{mgh}\right)}$. Thus the equivalent simple pendulum has length $\dfrac{I}{mh}$.

Alternatively, for a rigid body with radius of gyration k about a parallel axis through its centre of mass G,

$$T = 2\pi\sqrt{\left[\frac{k^2 + h^2}{gh}\right]}$$

and the equivalent simple pendulum has length

$$l = \frac{k^2 + h^2}{h}$$

Example 12

A uniform disc of radius a is performing small oscillations in a vertical plane about a smooth, horizontal axis which is perpendicular to the disc and passes through a point at a distance $\frac{a}{2}$ from its centre. Find the length of the simple equivalent pendulum.

M.I. of disc about axis through its centre $= \frac{1}{2}ma^2$

So: M.I. of disc about axis $\dfrac{a}{2}$ from its centre

$$= \tfrac{1}{2}ma^2 + m\left(\frac{a}{2}\right)^2$$

$$= \frac{3ma^2}{4}$$

And: length of simple equivalent pendulum $= \dfrac{I}{mh}$

$$= \frac{3ma^2}{4} \times \frac{1}{m \times \dfrac{a}{2}}$$

$$= \frac{3a}{2}$$

Exercise 2D

Calculate (i) the period of small oscillations about their equilibrium positions.

and   (ii) the length of the simple equivalent pendulum

for each of the bodies in questions 1–6 with rotation about the given axes.

1   A uniform rod of mass m and length $2a$, axis through one end, perpendicular to the rod.

2   A uniform rod of mass m and length $2a$ with a particle of mass $3m$ attached at one end, axis through the other end, perpendicular to the rod.

3 A uniform circular hoop of mass $2m$ and diameter d, axis through a point on the hoop, perpendicular to the plane of the hoop.

4 A triangular framework formed by joining three uniform rods each of length $2a$ and mass m at their ends, axis through a vertex of the triangle perpendicular to the plane of the triangle.

5 A uniform rectangular lamina of mass $3\,\text{kg}$ measuring $2\,\text{m}$ by $4\,\text{m}$, axis coinciding with a short side of the lamina.

6 A uniform circular disc, centre O, mass m and radius r, with a particle mass m attached at A where $OA = \dfrac{r}{2}$, axis through O perpendicular to the disc.

7 A uniform rod AB of length $2a$ and mass m is free to rotate about a fixed, smooth, horizontal axis through A. Find the period of small oscillations of the rod. A particle is now attached to end B of the rod and as a result the period of small oscillations is increased by 20%. Find the mass of the particle.

8 A pendulum consists of a uniform rod, of mass M and length $2a$, pivoted at its mid-point O and a small nut of mass m which can be screwed to any point of the rod.

(a) Find the period T of a small oscillation in a vertical plane when the nut is a distance x from O.

(b) Show that if $3m < M$ then T decreases as x increases.

(c) When $3m > M$ find the value of x which makes T a minimum.

9 A thin uniform rod AB of mass m and length $6a$, can turn freely in a vertical plane about a smooth, horizontal axis through end A. A uniform circular disc of mass $12m$ and radius a, is clamped to the rod so that its plane coincides with the plane in which the rod can turn.

(a) Show that for different positions of the disc the minimum length of the equivalent simple pendulum is $2a$.

(b) Find the maximum length of the equivalent simple pendulum.

10 The figure shows a compound pendulum which consists of a uniform solid sphere of mass m and radius a attached to a uniform rod of mass $\frac{1}{4}m$ and length $2a$. They are attached so that the centre of the sphere lies on the rod produced and so is a distance $3a$ from the pivot O. Find the moment of inertia of the system about a horizontal axis through O and hence the length of the equivalent simple pendulum.

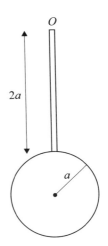

SUMMARY OF KEY POINTS

1 The kinetic energy of a rigid body which is rotating with angular speed $\dot{\theta}$ is given by

$$\text{K.E.} = \tfrac{1}{2} I \dot{\theta}^2$$

where I is the moment of inertia of the body about the axis of rotation.

2 When a rigid body is rotating, the gain in potential energy of the body is given by

$$\text{Gain in P.E.} = mgh$$

where m is the mass of the body and h is the vertical height gained by its centre of mass.

3 When a rigid body is rotating about a smooth axis with no external forces acting on the body, the sum of the kinetic and potential energies of the body will remain constant.

4 The equation of rotational motion states:

$$L = I\ddot{\theta}$$

where L is the moment about the axis of rotation of the resultant force on the rotating body, I is the moment of inertia of the body about the axis of rotation and $\ddot{\theta}$ is the angular acceleration of the body.

5 For a rigid body which is rotating about a fixed, smooth axis, the force exerted by the axis on the body can be calculated by considering the motion of a particle of the same mass as the body placed at the centre of mass of the body under the action of the same forces as those acting on the body.

6 The angular momentum of a rigid body rotating with angular speed $\dot{\theta}$ is given by

$$\text{Angular momentum} = I\dot{\theta}$$

7 When there are no external forces with moments about the axis of rotation acting on a system the total angular momentum of the system remains constant.

8 For a rigid body performing small oscillations about a fixed, horizontal axis (a compound pendulum) the period of oscillations is

$$2\pi\sqrt{\left(\frac{I}{mgh}\right)}$$

where I is the moment of inertia of the body about the axis, m is the mass of the body and h is the distance of the centre of mass of the body from the axis.

9 For a rigid body performing small oscillations about a fixed horizontal axis, the period of oscillations is

$$2\pi\sqrt{\left[\frac{k^2 + h^2}{gh}\right]}$$

where h is the distance of the centre of mass from the axis and k is the radius of gyration of the body about a parallel axis through the centre of mass.

10 The simple pendulum which has the same period as a given compound pendulum is called the equivalent simple pendulum. It has length

$$\frac{I}{mh} \quad \text{or} \quad \frac{k^2 + h^2}{h}$$

Review exercise 1

1 Given that the moment of inertia of a uniform disc, of radius a and mass m, about an axis through its centre perpendicular to its plane is $\frac{1}{2}ma^2$, obtain the moment of inertia about a diameter of the disc.

Hence obtain the moment of inertia about a tangent to the disc in the plane of the disc. [L]

2 Show, by integration, that the moment of inertia of a uniform rod, of length $2l$ and mass m, about an axis through its centre and perpendicular to the rod is $\frac{1}{3}ml^2$.

A uniform square plate, of mass M, has edges of length $2a$. Find the moment of inertia of this plate about an axis through its centre perpendicular to the plane of the plate. [L]

3 A uniform circular disc of radius $2a$ has a concentric hole of radius a. The mass of the annulus is M. Find the moment of inertia of the annulus about an axis through a point on the circumference of the circle of radius a
   (a) if the axis is perpendicular to the plane of the annulus
   (b) if the axis lies in the plane of the annulus and touches the circle. [L]

4 A uniform circular plate of diameter 5 m has a hole of diameter 1 m punched in it. The centre of the hole is 1.5 m from the centre of the plate. Calculate the radius of gyration of the plate
   (a) about the diameter through the centre of the hole
   (b) about the diameter which is perpendicular to this.

5 A uniform square lamina $ABCD$ of mass m and side $2a$ is free to rotate in a vertical plane about an axis through its centre O perpendicular to the plane of the lamina. Particles each of mass m are attached to points A and B of the lamina. The system is

released from rest with AB vertical. Show that the angular speed of the system when AB is horizontal is $\sqrt{\left(\dfrac{6g}{7a}\right)}$.

6 A uniform disc, of mass $2m$ and radius r, is free to rotate about a smooth horizontal axis passing through the centre of the disc and perpendicular to the plane of the disc. A light inextensible string, attached to the rim of the disc, passes round part of the rim and then vertically downwards to a hanging particle P of mass $3m$ to which the other end of the string is attached. The system starts from rest. Find the distance that P has fallen when it has acquired a speed V, assuming that some of the string is still wound round the rim. Find also the acceleration of P and the tension in that part of the string which is hanging vertically.

[L]

7 A uniform circular disc of mass 12 kg and radius 10 cm is free to rotate about a horizontal axis through its centre perpendicular to its plane. A particle of mass 3 kg is attached to the highest point of the rim of the disc and the equilibrium of the system is slightly disturbed. Find the angular speed of the particle, in revolutions per minute, when the particle is passing through its lowest point. [L]

8 A wheel has a cord of length 10 m coiled round its axle; the cord is pulled with a constant force of 100 N and when the cord leaves the axle the wheel is rotating 5 times a second. Calculate the moment of inertia of the wheel and axle. [L]

9 Three equal uniform rods, each of length l and mass m, form the sides of an equilateral triangle ABC. The triangular frame is attached to a smooth hinge at A, about which it can rotate in a vertical plane. The frame is held, with AB horizontal and C below AB, and then let go from rest. Find the maximum angular speed of the triangle in the subsequent motion. [L]

10 A bucket of mass m hangs at the end of a light rope which is coiled round a wheel of mass M. If the wheel can rotate freely about its axis, which is horizontal, and if its entire mass is supposed concentrated in its rim, find the speed of the bucket when it has fallen a distance x from rest. [L]

11 A uniform wire of mass M and length $4a$ is bent in the form of a square. It is hung by one corner over a smooth horizontal nail and released from rest from the position in which the sides are horizontal and vertical and the centre of mass is at a lower level than the nail. Find the angular speed with which it passes through the position in which the diagonals are horizontal and vertical and the resultant reaction on the nail as it passes through this position.   [L]

12 Find the moment of inertia of a uniform square lamina $ABCD$, of side $2a$ and mass m, about an axis through A perpendicular to the plane of the lamina.

The lamina is free to rotate about a fixed smooth horizontal axis through A perpendicular to the plane of the lamina. Show that its period of small oscillations about the stable equilibrium position is

$$2\pi\left(\frac{8a}{3g\sqrt{2}}\right)^{\frac{1}{2}}$$

The lamina is rotating with angular speed ω when C is vertically below A. Determine the components, along and perpendicular to AC, of the reaction of the lamina on the axis when AC makes an angle θ with the downward vertical through A.   [L]

13 A thin uniform rod, of length $2a$ and mass M, attached to a smooth fixed hinge at one end O is allowed to fall from a horizontal position. Show that in the subsequent motion

$$2a\left(\frac{\mathrm{d}\theta}{\mathrm{d}t}\right)^2 = 3g\sin\theta$$

where θ is the angle made by the rod with the horizontal. Find, in terms of M, g and θ, the resolved parts, along the rod and perpendicular to the rod, of the force exerted by the rod on the axis of rotation.

Show that the resolved part of this force in a horizontal direction is greatest when $\theta = \dfrac{\pi}{4}$ and that the resolved vertical part is then $\dfrac{11Mg}{8}$.   [L]

14 A uniform rod, of length $4a$ and mass m, is held at the edge of a horizontal table with a length a resting on the table at right angles to the edge and the remainder projecting beyond the table. The rod is released. Assuming that the edge of the table is rough enough to prevent slipping during rotation of the rod through an angle θ, find, in terms of m, g and θ, the reactions on the rod at the point of contact along and perpendicular to the rod.

Show that, if μ is the coefficient of friction, the rod will begin to slip when it has turned through an angle α given by

$$\tan \alpha = \frac{4\mu}{13}$$

[L]

15 Four uniform rods, each of mass m and length $2l$ are joined rigidly together to form a square frame $ABCD$ of side $2l$. The frame is placed with all four sides at rest on a smooth horizontal table. An inextensible string has one end attached at the corner A. A particle of mass $4m$ is tied to the other end of the string. The particle, initially at A, is projected with speed u in the direction DA. Given that the speed of the particle immediately after the string becomes taut is V, show that the initial angular speed of the square frame about an axis through its centre of gravity perpendicular to the plane of the frame is ω where $\omega = \frac{2V - u}{l}$. Show that $V = \frac{7u}{11}$ and that immediately after the string becomes taut the kinetic energy of the particle and frame is $\frac{14mu^2}{11}$.

[L]

16 A uniform rigid rod AB, of mass M and length $2a$ is falling freely without rotation under gravity with AB horizontal. Suddenly the end A is fixed when the speed of the rod is v. Find the angular speed with which the rod begins to rotate.   [L]

17 Find, by integration, the moment of inertia of a uniform circular disc, of mass M and radius a, about an axis which passes through the centre and is perpendicular to the plane of the disc.

Hence show that the moment of inertia of such a disc about a tangent line in its plane is $\frac{5Ma^2}{4}$.

The disc rotates about a fixed smooth horizontal axis which is the tangent to the disc at the point A. The centre O of the disc describes a vertical circle with centre A in a plane perpendicular to this tangent. The disc is released from rest when its plane is horizontal. Find the angular speed of the disc when it is first vertical.

At the instant when the disc is in this vertical position, it is hit at its centre by a particle of mass M, travelling with speed u in the direction of motion of the centre of the disc. Given that the particle adheres to the disc, find, in terms of u, a and g, the angular speed of the system immediately after impact. [L]

18 A rod AB, of length $2a$ and mass $2m$, lies at rest on a smooth horizontal table and is pivoted about a smooth vertical axis through A. A small body of mass m, moving on the table with speed V at right angles to the rod, strikes the rod at a distance d from A. Given that the body sticks to the rod after impact, find the angular speed with which the rod starts to move. [L]

19 To the end B of a thin uniform rod AB, of length $3a$ and mass m, is attached a thin uniform circular disc, of radius a and mass m, so that the rod and the diameter BC of the disc are in a straight line with $AC = 5a$. Show that the moment of inertia of this composite body about an axis through A perpendicular to AB and in the plane of the disc is $\dfrac{77ma^2}{4}$.

The body is held at rest with the end A smoothly hinged to a fixed pivot and with the plane of the disc *horizontal*. The body is released and has angular speed ω when AC is vertical. Find ω in terms of a and g.

When AC is vertical, the centre of the disc strikes a stationary particle of mass $\frac{1}{2}m$. Given that the particle adheres to the centre of the disc, show that the angular speed of the body immediately after impact is $\dfrac{77\omega}{109}$.

20 Show, by integration, that the moment of inertia of a uniform circular disc, of mass M and radius a, about an axis which passes through its centre and is perpendicular to its plane is $\dfrac{Ma^2}{2}$.

Without further integration, deduce the moment of inertia of the disc

(a) about an axis perpendicular to its plane and passing through a point on its circumference

(b) about a diameter.

A uniform disc, of mass M and radius a, is suspended from a smooth pivot at a point on its circumference and rests in equilibrium. Calculate the period of small oscillations when the centre of the disc is slightly displaced

(c) in the plane of the disc,

(d) perpendicular to the plane of the disc. [L]

21 A compound pendulum consists of a thin uniform rod AB, of length $2a$ and mass $3m$, with a particle mass $2m$ attached at B. The pendulum is free to rotate in a vertical plane about a horizontal axis perpendicular to the rod through a point C of the rod at a distance $x(< a)$ from A. Show that the moment of inertia of the pendulum about this axis through C is

$$(5x^2 - 14ax + 12a^2)m$$

Find the square of the period of small oscillations of the pendulum. Show that, as x varies, the period takes its minimum value when $x = \dfrac{[7 - \sqrt{(11)}]a}{5}$. [L]

22 Use integration to show that the moment of inertia of a uniform sphere, of mass m and radius a, about a diameter is $\frac{2}{5}ma^2$. Hence, or otherwise, find the moment of inertia of the sphere about a tangent.

The sphere is free to rotate about a fixed horizontal tangent line with its centre O moving in a vertical plane perpendicular to the tangent. Show that, when the sphere oscillates about the position of stable equilibrium, its equation of motion is the same as that of a simple pendulum of length $\dfrac{7a}{5}$.

Given that the sphere oscillates between the positions in which O is on the same horizontal level as the tangential axis, find the maximum speed of O during the motion. [L]

23 Show, by integration, that the moment of inertia of a thin uniform circular disc of radius a and mass m, about an axis through the centre of the disc perpendicular to the plane of the disc is $\frac{1}{2}ma^2$.

Hence determine the moment of inertia of the disc about a parallel axis through a point on the rim of the disc.

This disc is free to rotate in a fixed vertical plane about a fixed horizontal axis through a point on the rim of the disc and at right angles to the plane of the disc. The diameter through the axis makes an angle θ with the downward vertical. Given that the disc is released from rest when $\theta = \frac{\pi}{2}$, find the speed of the centre of the disc as the centre passes through its lowest point.

In another situation when the disc is at rest with its centre vertically below the axis, it is given a small horizontal impulse acting in the plane of the disc. Show that the motion is approximately simple harmonic and find the period of the motion.   [L]

24 A uniform rod AB, of length $2a$ and mass $6m$, has a particle of mass $2m$ attached at B. The rod is free to rotate in a vertical plane about a smooth fixed horizontal axis perpendicular to the rod and passing through a point X of the rod so that $AX = x$, where $x < a$. Show that the moment of inertia of the system about this axis is

$$4m(4a^2 - 5ax + 2x^2)$$

Find the period of small oscillations of the system about its equilibrium position with B below A.   [L]

25. Prove, by integration, that the moment of inertia of a uniform rod of mass m and length a, about an axis through its mid-point and perpendicular to the rod is $\dfrac{ma^2}{12}$.

Four uniform rods AB, BC, CD and DA, each of length a, are rigidly joined to form a square $ABCD$. Each of the rods AB, CD and DA has mass m and rod BC has mass $3m$. The rods are free to rotate about a smooth horizontal axis, L, which passes through A and is perpendicular to the plane of the square.

(a) Show that the moment of inertia of the system about L is $6ma^2$ and find the distance of the centre of mass of the system from A.

The system is released from rest with AB horizontal and C vertically below B.

(b) Find the greatest value of the angular speed of the system in the subsequent motion.

(c) Find the period of small oscillations of the system about the position of stable equilibrium. [L]

26 Show that the moment of inertia of a uniform solid right circular cone, of mass m, height h and base radius a, about a line through its vertex and perpendicular to its axis of symmetry is

$$\frac{3m(a^2 + 4h^2)}{20}$$

[You may assume that the moment of inertia of a uniform circular disc, of mass M and radius R, about a diameter is $\frac{MR^2}{4}$].

A cone, with $h = \frac{2a}{3}$, is free to rotate about a smooth horizontal axis through its vertex. Find the period of small oscillations under gravity about the stable position of equilibrium. [L]

27 A uniform lamina, of mass m, has the form of a quadrant of a circle of radius a. Show, by integration, that the moment of inertia of the lamina, about an axis l perpendicular to the plane of the lamina and through the centre of the circle of which it is part, is $\frac{1}{2}ma^2$.

The lamina is free to rotate about the axis l, which is horizontal and when the centre of mass of the lamina is vertically below the axis of rotation the angular speed is Ω. Determine whether the lamina makes complete revolutions in the cases

(a) $\Omega = 2\sqrt{\left(\frac{g}{a}\right)}$.

(b) $\Omega = 3\sqrt{\left(\frac{g}{a}\right)}$.

If the lamina is given a small displacement from its position of stable equilibrium, find the period of its motion as a compound pendulum.

[You may assume that the centre of mass of the lamina is at a distance $\dfrac{4\sqrt{2}a}{3\pi}$ from the axis of rotation.]   [L]

28 Prove that the moment of inertia of a uniform solid sphere of mass M and radius a about a diameter is $\dfrac{2Ma^2}{5}$. Deduce that the radius of gyration of a uniform solid hemisphere of radius a about any axis through the centre of its plane face is $a\sqrt{\tfrac{2}{5}}$.

Two identical uniform solid hemispheres are such that one can rotate freely about its axis of symmetry, which is fixed, and the other can rotate freely about a fixed axis which coincides with a tangent to the circular rim of its plane face. Find the ratio of their angular speeds when their kinetic energies are equal.   [L]

Further motion of particles in one dimension

In Books M1 and M2 you studied the kinematics of a particle moving in a straight line. In Book M1 the case of constant acceleration was dealt with. This was generalised in Book M2 to situations where the acceleration is a function of the displacement (x) or time (t). Now we are going to consider the case where the acceleration is a function of the speed (v).

In much of the modelling dealt with in Books M1 and M2 we assumed that air resistance could be neglected. But air resistance in many circumstances is *not* negligible and is not constant. In fact the magnitude of the resistance depends on the speed of the particle and is usually taken to be proportional to the speed for low speeds and proportional to the square of the speed for higher speeds. So when air resistance is taken into acount the acceleration will be a function of the speed. We will consider only circumstances in which the acceleration is either

$$a + bv, \text{ where } a \text{ and } b \text{ are constants}$$

or

$$\alpha + \beta v^2, \text{ where } \alpha \text{ and } \beta \text{ are constants.}$$

3.1 Kinematics of a particle moving in a straight line when the acceleration is a function of speed

Consider a particle P moving in a straight line. Suppose that at time t seconds the displacement of P from a fixed point O in the line is x metres, its velocity is $v\,\mathrm{m\,s^{-1}}$ and its acceleration is $a\,\mathrm{m\,s^{-2}}$.

You should recall from chapter 1 of Book M2 that

(i) $$a = \frac{\mathrm{d}v}{\mathrm{d}t}$$

and (ii) $$a = v\frac{\mathrm{d}v}{\mathrm{d}x} = \frac{\mathrm{d}}{\mathrm{d}x}(\tfrac{1}{2}v^2)$$

When a is a function of v:

$$a = \mathrm{f}(v)$$

so, using (i): $$\frac{\mathrm{d}v}{\mathrm{d}t} = \mathrm{f}(v)$$

Integrating: $$\int \frac{\mathrm{d}v}{\mathrm{f}(v)} = \int \mathrm{d}t$$

or $$t = \int \frac{\mathrm{d}v}{\mathrm{f}(v)} + c \qquad (1)$$

where c is an arbitrary constant of integration.

Alternatively, using (ii):

$$v\frac{\mathrm{d}v}{\mathrm{d}x} = \mathrm{f}(v)$$

Integrating: $$\int \frac{v\,\mathrm{d}v}{\mathrm{f}(v)} = \int \mathrm{d}x$$

or $$x = \int \frac{v\,\mathrm{d}v}{\mathrm{f}(v)} + k \qquad (2)$$

where k is an arbitrary constant of integration.

When you do the integration over v in equation (2), you get:

$$x = \mathrm{F}(v) + k \qquad (3)$$

In some cases you may be able, by writing $v = \dfrac{\mathrm{d}x}{\mathrm{d}t}$, to integrate (3) to obtain a relationship between x and t.

Example 1

A particle P is moving along Ox with an acceleration of $-(9 + v^2)\,\mathrm{m\,s^{-2}}$ at time t seconds when its displacement from O is x metres and its speed is $v\,\mathrm{m\,s^{-1}}$. When $t = 0$, $x = 0$ and $v = u$. Find the value of t and the value of x when the particle comes to rest.

Using: $$a = \frac{\mathrm{d}v}{\mathrm{d}t} = -(9 + v^2)$$

gives: $$\int \frac{dv}{9 + v^2} = -t + c$$

Integrating: $$\tfrac{1}{3}\arctan\left(\frac{v}{3}\right) = -t + c$$

(See Book P3, chapter 5.)

Substituting $v = u$ when $t = 0$ gives:

$$c = \tfrac{1}{3}\arctan\left(\frac{u}{3}\right)$$

So: $$t = \tfrac{1}{3}\arctan\left(\frac{u}{3}\right) - \tfrac{1}{3}\arctan\left(\frac{v}{3}\right)$$

The particles comes to rest when $v = 0$. Then:

$$t = \tfrac{1}{3}\arctan\left(\frac{u}{3}\right)$$

Using: $$a = v\frac{dv}{dx} = -(9 + v^2)$$

gives: $$\int \frac{v\,dv}{(9 + v^2)} = -x + k$$

Integrating: $$\tfrac{1}{2}\ln(9 + v^2) = -x + k$$

Substituting $v = u$ when $x = 0$ gives

$$k = \tfrac{1}{2}\ln(9 + u^2)$$

So: $$x = \tfrac{1}{2}\ln(9 + u^2) - \tfrac{1}{2}\ln(9 + v^2)$$

The particle comes to rest when $v = 0$.

So: $$x = \tfrac{1}{2}\ln(9 + u^2) - \tfrac{1}{2}\ln 9$$
$$= \tfrac{1}{2}\ln\left(1 + \frac{u^2}{9}\right)$$

Example 2

A particle P is moving along Ox with an acceleration of $-(5 + 2v)$ m s^{-2} at time t seconds when its displacement from O is x metres and its speed is v m s^{-1}. When $t = 0$, $x = 0$ and $v = 10$. Find the value of t and the value of x when $v = 5$.

Using $$a = \frac{dv}{dt} = -(5 + 2v)$$

gives: $$\int \frac{dv}{5 + 2v} = -t + c$$

Integrating: $\qquad \frac{1}{2}\ln(5+2v) = -t+c$

Substituting $v = 10$ when $t = 0$ gives:

$$c = \tfrac{1}{2}\ln(25)$$

So: $\qquad t = \tfrac{1}{2}\ln(25) - \tfrac{1}{2}\ln(5+2v)$

When $v = 5$,

$$t = \tfrac{1}{2}\ln 25 - \tfrac{1}{2}\ln(5+10)$$
$$= \tfrac{1}{2}\ln(\tfrac{25}{15})$$
$$= \tfrac{1}{2}\ln(\tfrac{5}{3}) = 0.255$$

Using: $\qquad a = v\dfrac{\mathrm{d}v}{\mathrm{d}x} = -(5+2v)$

gives: $\qquad \displaystyle\int \frac{v\,\mathrm{d}v}{5+2v} = -x+k$

To integrate the left-hand side, divide out to obtain:

$$\int \left[\frac{1}{2} - \frac{\frac{5}{2}}{(5+2v)} \right] \mathrm{d}v$$

Integrating: $\qquad \frac{1}{2}v - \frac{5}{2} \times \frac{1}{2}\ln(5+2v) = -x+k$

Substituting $v = 10$ when $x = 0$ gives:

$$k = \tfrac{1}{2}(10) - \tfrac{5}{4}\ln(5+2\times10)$$
$$= 5 - \tfrac{5}{4}\ln(25)$$

So: $\qquad x = 5 - \tfrac{5}{4}\ln(25) - \tfrac{1}{2}v + \tfrac{5}{4}\ln(5+2v)$

When $v = 5$,

$$x = 5 - \tfrac{5}{4}\ln(25) - \tfrac{1}{2}(5) + \tfrac{5}{4}\ln(15)$$
$$= 2\tfrac{1}{2} - \tfrac{5}{4}\ln(\tfrac{5}{3})$$
$$= 1.86$$

So when $v = 5$, $t = 0.255\,\mathrm{s}$ and $x = 1.86\,\mathrm{m}$.

3.2 Vertical motion taking into account air resistance

Resistance proportional to speed

Consider a particle P of mass m and suppose the air resistance is of magnitude mkv, where v is the speed and k is a positive constant.

(i) Particle falling from rest at a point O

Measure the displacement *downwards* from O, because O is a **fixed point**.

■ **Displacements must always be measured from a fixed point.**

The forces acting on the particle are its weight mg and the resistance, as shown in the diagram. The equation of motion is

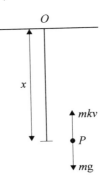

$$m \times \text{acceleration} = mg - mkv$$

So:

$$\text{acceleration} = a = g - kv$$

Using $a = \dfrac{dv}{dt}$ gives:

$$\frac{dv}{dt} = g - kv \qquad (1)$$

Integrating:

$$\int \frac{dv}{g - kv} = t + c$$

So:

$$-\frac{1}{k}\ln(g - kv) = t + c$$

Substituting $v = 0$ when $t = 0$ gives:

$$c = -\frac{1}{k}\ln g$$

and

$$t = \frac{1}{k}\ln g - \frac{1}{k}\ln(g - kv) = \frac{1}{k}\ln\left(\frac{g}{g - kv}\right)$$

Hence:

$$e^{kt} = \frac{g}{g - kv}$$

or:

$$(g - kv) = ge^{-kt}$$

so that:

$$v = \frac{g}{k}(1 - e^{-kt}) \qquad (2)$$

Since

$$\lim_{t \to \infty}(1 - e^{-kt}) = 1$$

the speed v tends to $\dfrac{g}{k}$. This is called the **terminal velocity**.

If you substitute this value in the differential equation you get:

$$a = \frac{\mathrm{d}v}{\mathrm{d}t} = g - kv$$

$$= g - k\frac{g}{k}$$

$$= g - g$$

$$= 0$$

So if and when v reached the value $\frac{g}{k}$ the acceleration would become zero and the particle would then descend with *uniform* speed. This is a plot of v against t:

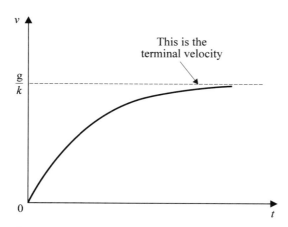

Using $a = v\dfrac{\mathrm{d}v}{\mathrm{d}x}$ gives:

$$v\frac{\mathrm{d}v}{\mathrm{d}x} = g - kv$$

Integrating:

$$\int \frac{v\,\mathrm{d}v}{g - kv} = x + A$$

To carry out the integration over v we write

$$v = -\frac{1}{k}(g - kv) + \frac{g}{k}$$

as $(g - kv)$ occurs in the denominator. Using this gives

$$\int \left(-\frac{1}{k} + \frac{g}{k}\frac{1}{(g - kv)}\right)\mathrm{d}v = x + A$$

Integrating over v gives

$$-\frac{1}{k}v - \frac{g}{k^2}\ln(g - kv) = x + A$$

But $v = 0$ when $x = 0$.

So:
$$A = -\frac{g}{k^2} \ln g$$

and
$$x = \frac{g}{k^2} \ln\left(\frac{g}{g - kv}\right) - \frac{v}{k}$$

In this case you can integrate equation (2) to obtain x as a function of t.

From (2):
$$v = \frac{dx}{dt} = \frac{g}{k}\left(1 - e^{-kt}\right)$$

Integrating:
$$x = \frac{gt}{k} + \frac{g}{k^2} e^{-kt} + C$$

But $x = 0$ when $t = 0$

So:
$$C = -\frac{g}{k^2}$$

and
$$x = \frac{g}{k^2}\left(kt + e^{-kt} - 1\right)$$

(ii) Particle projected vertically upwards with speed U

This time, measure the displacement *upwards* from the point of projection O', since O' is a fixed point. The forces acting on the particle are shown in the diagram. If the speed of the particle is u, then the equation of motion is

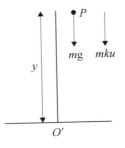

$$a = -g - ku$$

Using $a = \dfrac{du}{dt}$ gives:

$$\frac{du}{dt} = -g - ku$$

Integrating:
$$\int \frac{du}{g + ku} = -t + c$$

So:
$$\frac{1}{k} \ln(g + ku) = -t + c$$

Substituting $u = U$ when $t = 0$ gives:

$$c = \frac{1}{k} \ln(g + kU)$$

so that
$$\frac{1}{k} \ln(g + ku) - \frac{1}{k} \ln(g + kU) = -t$$

and
$$t = \frac{1}{k} \ln\left(\frac{g + kU}{g + ku}\right)$$

You can find the time the particle takes to reach the highest point of the path by setting $u = 0$.

So:
$$\text{time} = \frac{1}{k} \ln\left(1 + \frac{kU}{g}\right)$$

Using $a = u \dfrac{du}{dy}$ gives

$$u \frac{du}{dy} = -g - ku$$

Integrating:
$$\int \frac{u\, du}{g + ku} = -y + A$$

or:
$$\frac{1}{k} \int \left(1 - \frac{g}{g + ku}\right) du = -y + A$$

So:
$$\frac{1}{k} u - \frac{g}{k^2} \ln(g + ku) = -y + A$$

Substituting: $u = U$ when $y = 0$ gives:

$$A = \frac{1}{k} U - \frac{g}{k^2} \ln(g + kU)$$

So:
$$y = \frac{1}{k}(U - u) + \frac{g}{k^2} \ln\left(\frac{g + ku}{g + kU}\right)$$

You can find the greatest height h that the particle reaches by setting $u = 0$. Thus:

$$h = \frac{1}{k} U + \frac{g}{k^2} \ln\left(\frac{g}{g + kU}\right)$$

Resistance proportional to the square of the speed

Consider a particle P of mass m subject to a resistance of magnitude mkv^2, where v is the speed and k is a positive constant.

(i) Particle falling from rest at a point O

As before, measure the displacement downwards from O. The forces now acting on the particle are shown in the diagram. The equation of motion is:

$$m \times \text{acceleration} = mg - mkv^2$$

First notice that if and when v reaches the value $\sqrt{\left(\frac{g}{k}\right)}$ the

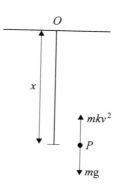

acceleration would become zero and P would continue to descend with constant speed $\sqrt{\left(\frac{g}{k}\right)}$. In what follows, therefore, you can assume that $v < \sqrt{\left(\frac{g}{k}\right)}$.

Using $a = \dfrac{dv}{dt}$ gives:

$$\frac{dv}{dt} = g - kv^2$$

Integrating:

$$\int \frac{dv}{g - kv^2} = t + c$$

You can write the left-hand side of this equation as partial fractions (see **Book P2, chapter 1**). It becomes

$$\frac{1}{k} \times \frac{1}{2\sqrt{\left(\frac{g}{k}\right)}} \int \left[\frac{1}{\sqrt{\left(\frac{g}{k}\right)} + v} + \frac{1}{\sqrt{\left(\frac{g}{k}\right)} - v} \right] dv$$

$$= \frac{1}{2\sqrt{(kg)}} \ln \left[\frac{\sqrt{\left(\frac{g}{k}\right)} + v}{\sqrt{\left(\frac{g}{k}\right)} - v} \right]$$

So:

$$\frac{1}{2\sqrt{(kg)}} \ln \left[\frac{\sqrt{\left(\frac{g}{k}\right)} + v}{\sqrt{\left(\frac{g}{k}\right)} - v} \right] = t + c$$

Substituting $v = 0$ when $t = 0$ gives $c = 0$, and so:

$$\frac{1}{2\sqrt{(kg)}} \ln \left(\frac{\sqrt{\left(\frac{g}{k}\right)} + v}{\sqrt{\left(\frac{g}{k}\right)} - v} \right) = t$$

or:

$$\left(\frac{\sqrt{\left(\frac{g}{k}\right)} + v}{\sqrt{\left(\frac{g}{k}\right)} - v} \right) = e^{2t\sqrt{(kg)}}$$

so that:

$$e^{2t\sqrt{(kg)}} \left(\sqrt{\left(\frac{g}{k}\right)} - v \right) = \sqrt{\left(\frac{g}{k}\right)} + v$$

Solving for v:

$$v = \sqrt{\left(\frac{g}{k}\right)}\left[\frac{e^{2t\sqrt{(kg)}} - 1}{e^{2t\sqrt{(kg)}} + 1}\right]$$

or:

$$v = \sqrt{\left(\frac{g}{k}\right)}\left[\frac{1 - e^{-2t\sqrt{(kg)}}}{1 + e^{-2t\sqrt{(kg)}}}\right]$$

As $t \to \infty$ the speed $v \to \sqrt{\left(\frac{g}{k}\right)}$ which is called the **terminal speed**
of the particle, or sometimes, rather loosely, the terminal velocity.
Here is a plot of v against t:

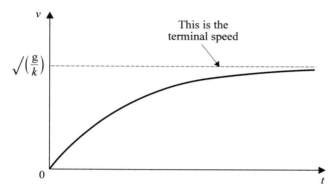

Using $a = v\dfrac{dv}{dx}$ gives:

$$v\frac{dv}{dx} = g - kv^2$$

Integrating:

$$\int \frac{v\,dv}{g - kv^2} = x + A$$

$$-\frac{1}{2k}\ln(g - kv^2) = x + A$$

(No modulus sign is required because $v < \sqrt{\left(\frac{g}{k}\right)}$.)

Substituting $x = 0$ when $v = 0$ gives:

$$A = -\frac{1}{2k}\ln g$$

and so:

$$x = \frac{1}{2k}\ln\left(\frac{g}{g - kv^2}\right)$$

or
$$v^2 = \frac{g}{k}(1 - e^{-2kx})$$

(ii) Particle projected vertically upwards with speed U

As before, measure the displacement *upwards* from the point of projection O'. The forces acting on the particle are shown in the diagram.

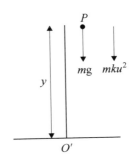

The speed of the particle is $u\,\text{m s}^{-1}$ and the equation of motion is:

$$a = -g - ku^2$$

Using $a = \dfrac{du}{dt}$ gives:

$$\frac{du}{dt} = -g - ku^2$$

Integrating:

$$\int \frac{du}{g + ku^2} = -t + c$$

or

$$\frac{1}{k}\int \frac{du}{\left(\dfrac{g}{k}\right) + u^2} = -t + c$$

$\Rightarrow$

$$\frac{1}{\sqrt{(kg)}} \arctan\left[u\sqrt{\left(\frac{k}{g}\right)}\right] = -t + c$$

Since $u = U$ when $t = 0$:

$$c = \frac{1}{\sqrt{(kg)}} \arctan\left[U\sqrt{\left(\frac{k}{g}\right)}\right]$$

So:

$$\sqrt{(kg)}\,t = \arctan\left[U\sqrt{\left(\frac{k}{g}\right)}\right] - \arctan\left[u\sqrt{\left(\frac{k}{g}\right)}\right]$$

The time T that particle P takes to reach the highest point of its path is obtained by substituting $u = 0$

So:

$$T = \frac{1}{\sqrt{(kg)}} \arctan\left[U\sqrt{\left(\frac{k}{g}\right)}\right]$$

Using $a = u\dfrac{du}{dy}$ gives:

$$u\frac{du}{dy} = -g - ku^2$$

Integrating:
$$\int \frac{u\,du}{g + ku^2} = -y + A$$

$$\frac{1}{2k} \ln(g + ku^2) = -y + A$$

Substituting $u = U$ when $y = 0$ gives:

$$A = \frac{1}{2k} \ln(g + kU^2)$$

and:
$$y = \frac{1}{2k} \ln\left[\frac{g + kU^2}{g + ku^2}\right]$$

You can find the greatest height H reached by the particle by substituting $u = 0$.

So:
$$H = \frac{1}{2k} \ln\left[1 + \frac{kU^2}{g}\right]$$

3.3 Resisted motion of a vehicle whose engine is working at a constant rate

In Book M1, chapter 5, we considered the motion of vehicles when the resistance to their movement was constant. This work can now be extended to the case where the resistance is a function of the speed of the vehicle.

Consider a vehicle of mass $m\,\text{kg}$ moving along a horizontal road with its engine working at the constant rate $h\,\text{W}$. Suppose the car is subject to a resistance $\text{f}(v)\,\text{N}$ where $v\,\text{m s}^{-1}$ is the speed of the vehicle. The tractive force $F\,\text{N}$ can be obtained from

$$F \times v = h$$

or:
$$F = \frac{h}{v}$$

So the equation of motion of the vehicle is

$$ma = F - \text{f}(v)$$
$$= \frac{h}{v} - \text{f}(v)$$

(i) Using: $a = \dfrac{dv}{dt}$

gives:
$$m\frac{dv}{dt} = \frac{h}{v} - \text{f}(v) \qquad (1)$$

(ii) Using: $a = v \dfrac{dv}{dx}$

gives:
$$mv \frac{dv}{dx} = \frac{h}{v} - f(v) \qquad (2)$$

If a relationship between v and t is required, use equation (1). If a relationship between v and x is required, use (2). The integration will depend on the function $f(v)$ and this is illustrated in the following example.

Example 3

A car of mass 560 kg moves along a straight road. The magnitude of the resistive force to the motion of the car is $80v$ N, where $v\,\text{m s}^{-1}$ is the speed of the car. The engine exerts a constant power of 72 kW.

(a) Find the time, in seconds, it takes for the car to accelerate from a speed of $10\,\text{m s}^{-1}$ to a speed of $20\,\text{m s}^{-1}$.

(b) Find the distance, in metres, that the car travels in this time.

(a) Since information is required regarding the time, use equation (1) with $f(v) = 80v$, $h = 72\,000$ and $m = 560$. The equation of motion is then

$$560 \frac{dv}{dt} = \frac{72\,000}{v} - 80v$$

or:
$$\frac{dv}{dt} = \frac{72\,000 - 80v^2}{560v}$$

$$= \frac{900 - v^2}{7v}$$

Separating the variables and integrating between $v = 10$ and $v = 20$ gives:

$$\int_{10}^{20} \frac{7v}{900 - v^2}\, dv = \int_0^T dt$$

or:
$$-\frac{7}{2}\left[\ln(900 - v^2) \right]_{10}^{20} = T$$

So:
$$T = \frac{7}{2} \ln\left[\frac{800}{500} \right] = \frac{7}{2} \ln\left(\frac{8}{5}\right) = 1.65 \text{ seconds}$$

It takes the car 1.65 seconds to accelerate from a speed of $10\,\text{m s}^{-1}$ to a speed of $20\,\text{m s}^{-1}$.

(b) Since you are asked to find the distance, use equation (2). The equation of motion is now

$$v \frac{dv}{dx} = \frac{900 - v^2}{7v}$$

Separating the variables and integrating between $v = 10$ and $v = 20$ gives:

$$\int_{10}^{20} \frac{7v^2}{900 - v^2} \, dv = \int_0^X dx = X$$

The left-hand side may be written as:

$$\int_{10}^{20} \left[-7 + \frac{6300}{900 - v^2} \right] dv$$

$$= \int_{10}^{20} \left[-7 + \frac{6300}{60} \left\{ \frac{1}{30 + v} + \frac{1}{30 - v} \right\} \right] dv$$

$$= \left[-7v + \frac{6300}{60} \ln \left(\frac{30 + v}{30 - v} \right) \right]_{10}^{20}$$

$$= -7(20 - 10) + 105 \ln \left(\frac{50}{10} \right) - 105 \ln \left(\frac{40}{20} \right)$$

$$= -70 + 105 \ln(\tfrac{5}{2})$$

So:
$$X = 26.2$$

The car travels 26.2 metres in this time.

Exercise 3A

1 A particle P is moving along Ox with an acceleration of $-(2 + v) \, m \, s^{-2}$ at time t seconds when its displacement from O is x metres and its speed is $v \, m \, s^{-1}$. When $t = 0$, $v = 12$.
   (a) Calculate the value of t when P comes to rest.
   (b) Calculate v when $t = 1.5$.

2 A particle P is moving along Ox with an acceleration of $-(4 + 3v) \, m \, s^{-2}$ at time t seconds, when its displacement from O is x metres and its speed is $v \, m \, s^{-1}$. When $x = 0$, $v = 4$. Calculate the value of x when P comes to rest.

3 A particle P is moving along Ox with an acceleration of $-(v^2 + 2) \, m \, s^{-2}$ at time t seconds when its displacement from O is x metres and its speed is $v \, m \, s^{-1}$. When $x = 0$, $v = 10$.
   (a) Find the distance travelled when $v = 0$.
   (b) Find the speed of P when $x = 1$.

4 A particle P of mass 2 kg is moving along Ox. At time t seconds the displacement of P from O is x metres and its speed is $v \, m \, s^{-1}$. The particle moves under the action of a retarding force

of magnitude $(12 + 3v^2)$ N. Initially, when $t = 0$, $x = 0$ and $v = 4$.

(a) Find the time taken by the particle to come to rest.

(b) Find the distance travelled in this time.

5 The retardation of a train with the power cut off is

$$\left(v^2 + \frac{u^2}{4} \right) \text{ms}^{-2}$$

where $v \, \text{m s}^{-1}$ is the speed and u is a constant.

Initially $v = u$.

(a) Show that the speed will be halved in a distance

$\frac{1}{2}\ln\left(\frac{5}{2}\right)$ metres in time $\frac{2}{u}\left[\arctan 2 - \frac{\pi}{4} \right]$ seconds.

(b) Show also that the train will come to rest in a further distance $\frac{1}{2}\ln 2$ metres in additional time $\frac{\pi}{2u}$ seconds.

6 A particle P of mass 1 kg is projected along a rough horizontal table with speed $u \, \text{m s}^{-1}$. The coefficient of friction between the particle and the surface is μ. The particle also suffers an air resistance of magnitude $9.8kv^2$ N when $v \, \text{m s}^{-1}$ is the speed of the particle and k is a constant. Find the distance travelled by P before it comes to rest and the time it takes to come to rest.

7 A ball of mass m is moving vertically under gravity. The air resistance is assumed to be mkv^2, where v is the speed of the ball and k is a constant. Initially the ball is projected downwards with a speed u where $u^2 < \frac{g}{k}$.

(a) Find the speed of the ball when it has fallen a distance d.

(b) Compare this with the value you would get for the speed of the ball at this point if you neglect air resistance.

8 A small stone of mass m moves in air in which the resistance to its motion varies as the square of the speed. The magnitude of the terminal speed is V. The ball is projected vertically upwards with a speed $V \tan \alpha$, where α is a constant.

(a) Show that the total energy, kinetic plus potential energy, lost in its ascent is

$$\tfrac{1}{2}mV^2(\tan^2 \alpha - 2\ln\sec\alpha)$$

(b) Show also that the stone will return to the point of projection with a speed $V \sin \alpha$.

9 A ball of mass m kg is projected vertically upwards with a speed of $19.6 \, \text{m s}^{-1}$ in a medium that subjects the ball to a resistance of magnitude $\frac{1}{2}mv$ where $v \, \text{m s}^{-1}$ is the speed of the ball.

(a) Show that t seconds after projection

$$v = 19.6(2e^{-t/2} - 1)$$

(b) Deduce that the ball reaches its maximum height $(\ln 4)$ seconds after projection.

10 A parachutist falls from rest from a balloon. Her parachute opens immediately and the air resistance with the parachute open is proportional to the speed of the parachutist. The terminal speed is $4 \, \text{m s}^{-1}$. Determine the distance the parachutist drops in the first 2 seconds of her fall.

11 A car of mass m is moving along a horizontal road with its engine working at an effective constant rate R. There is a resistance to the motion of the car of magnitude kv^2 where v is the speed of the car. Find the distance travelled by the car as its speed increases from $0.25\left(\dfrac{R}{k}\right)^{1/3}$ to $0.75\left(\dfrac{R}{k}\right)^{1/3}$

3.4 Damped simple harmonic motion

In chapter 2 of Book M2 you studied simple harmonic motion. This is motion along a straight line in which the force acting on the particle is directed towards a fixed point of the line and is proportional to the distance of the particle from that fixed point. If the fixed point is O, the distance x m of the particle, P, of mass m kg, from O satisfies the differential equation

$$m\ddot{x} = -m\omega^2 x$$

or: $$\ddot{x} = -\omega^2 x \qquad (1)$$

at time t seconds.

The general solution of equation (1) (see chapter 2 of Book M2) is

$$x = a\sin(\omega t + \alpha) \qquad (2)$$

where a and α are constants known as the amplitude and phase respectively. The graph of x against t is:

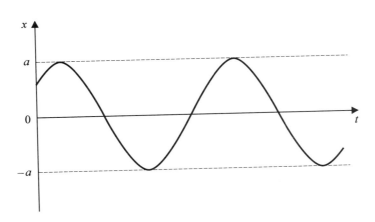

Section 2.6 of Book M2 studied the oscillations of a particle attached to one end of an elastic spring and moving on a smooth horizontal surface. We assumed there that the only horizontal force acting on the particle was the tension in the spring. The extension x of the spring then satisfies equation (1) with

$$\omega^2 = \frac{\lambda}{ml}$$

where l is the natural length and λ the modulus of the spring.

According to the graph above the particle will perform oscillations of constant amplitude. This is not what is observed in practice. The amplitude of the oscillations decreases in magnitude and they die out fairly quickly. The model must therefore be refined by taking into account other factors. The refinement to be considered here takes air resistance into account.

Consider now the situation where the particle suffers a resistance proportional to the speed $v\,\mathrm{m\,s^{-1}}$ in addition to the tension in the spring. Let the resistance be $mkv\,\mathrm{N}$. The equation of motion is now

$$m\,\frac{\mathrm{d}^2x}{\mathrm{d}t^2} = -m\omega^2 x - mk\,\frac{\mathrm{d}x}{\mathrm{d}t}$$

or:
$$\frac{\mathrm{d}^2x}{\mathrm{d}t^2} + k\,\frac{\mathrm{d}x}{\mathrm{d}t} + \omega^2 x = 0 \qquad (3)$$

This is a second order differential equation with constant coefficients. The solution of differential equations of this type is dealt with in chapter 8 of Book P3. The form of the solution depends on the relative values of k and ω^2. When k is small the motion is said to be **lightly damped**. When k is large the motion is said to be **heavily damped**.

You need to consider three separate cases, depending on whether k^2 is greater than, equal to, or less than $4\omega^2$. These correspond to the auxiliary equation for equation (3) having real distinct, equal, or complex roots.

Substituting $x = e^{\lambda t}$ into equation (3) gives

$$\lambda^2 + k\lambda + \omega^2 = 0 \tag{4}$$

(the auxiliary equation) so that $e^{\lambda t}$ is a solution provided that

$$\lambda = \frac{-k \pm \sqrt{(k^2 - 4\omega^2)}}{2}$$

(1) $k^2 > 4\omega^2$ (heavy damping).

There are two real distinct roots of equation (4) namely:

$$\lambda_1 = -\frac{k}{2} + \sqrt{\left(\frac{k^2}{4} - \omega^2\right)} < 0$$

and

$$\lambda_2 = -\frac{k}{2} - \sqrt{\left(\frac{k^2}{4} - \omega^2\right)} < 0$$

The general solution is now

$$x = Ae^{\lambda_1 t} + Be^{\lambda_2 t} \tag{5}$$

where A and B are arbitrary constants. Since both λ_1 and λ_2 are negative, both $e^{\lambda_1 t}$ and $e^{\lambda_2 t}$ *decrease to zero* as $t \to \infty$. The graph of x against t depends on the values of the constants A and B which in turn depend on the initial conditions, that is, the values of x and $\dot{x}$ when $t = 0$. The three possibilities are shown here:

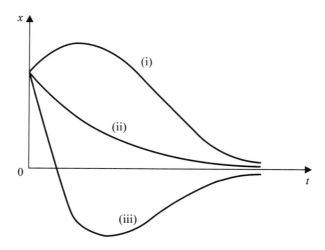

Example 4 will illustrate when each occurs.

(2) $k^2 = 4\omega^2$

The roots of the auxiliary equation are equal.

So:
$$\lambda_1 = \lambda_2 = -\frac{k}{2} = -\omega$$

and the general solution is

$$x = (\alpha + \beta t)e^{-\frac{1}{2}kt} = (\alpha + \beta t)e^{-\omega t} \qquad (6)$$

where α and β are arbitrary constants.

This has the same features as the solution in case (1). Again there are three possible cases (i), (ii) and (iii), depending on the initial conditions.

(3) $k^2 < 4\omega^2$ (light damping)

The roots are complex and:

$$\lambda_1 = -\frac{k}{2} + ip$$

$$\lambda_2 = -\frac{k}{2} - ip$$

where $p^2 = \omega^2 - \dfrac{k^2}{4}$.

The general solution can now be written in the form:

$$x = Ae^{-\frac{kt}{2}}\cos pt + Be^{-\frac{kt}{2}}\sin pt$$

or:
$$x = ae^{-\frac{kt}{2}}\cos(pt + \alpha) \qquad (7)$$

where A, B, a and α are arbitrary constants.

The graph of x against t is:

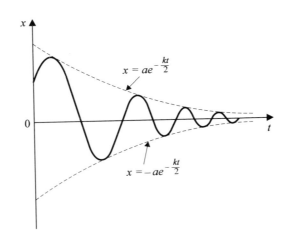

Since x lies between $\pm ae^{-\frac{kt}{2}}$ the graph of x lies between the two curves with equations $x = ae^{-\frac{kt}{2}}$ and $x = -ae^{-\frac{kt}{2}}$, which are also shown in the figure.

Notice the following points.

1. The motion is oscillatory, with the particle passing through the centre O, where $x = 0$, when $\cos(pt + \alpha) = 0$; that is, when $pt + \alpha$ is an odd integral multiple of $\dfrac{\pi}{2}$, that is $(2n + 1)\dfrac{\pi}{2}$. So these values of t occur at intervals of $\dfrac{\pi}{p}$.

The period of oscillation is the time to complete one oscillation. Here one complete oscillation is the path travelled by the particle in the interval of time between passing through O in the same direction on successive occasions. The period is then:

$$\frac{2\pi}{p} = \frac{2\pi}{\sqrt{\left(\omega^2 - \dfrac{k^2}{4}\right)}}$$

Compare this with the period of undamped simple harmonic motion, which is $\dfrac{2\pi}{\omega}$. The period of oscillation is therefore *lengthened* by the damping.

2. The maximum and minimum values of x occur when $\dfrac{dx}{dt} = 0$, that is when

$$\tfrac{1}{2} k \cos(pt + \alpha) + p \sin(pt + \alpha) = 0$$

or: $$\tan(pt + \alpha) = -\frac{k}{2p}$$

The maximum and minimum values therefore occur at intervals of $\dfrac{\pi}{p}$, since the tangent function is of period π (see chapter 7, Book P1).

It can be shown that their numerical values diminish in geometrical progression with common ratio $e^{-k\pi/2p}$ (see example 5). This case is of practical importance and the term 'damped harmonic motion' is often applied to it.

Example 4

A particle P of mass 1 kg moves in a horizontal straight line under the action of a force directed towards a fixed point O of the line. The force varies as the distance of the particle from O and is equal to $4x$ N when P is at a distance x metres from O. The particle is also subject to a resisting force which is proportional to its speed and which is equal to $5v\,\text{N}$ when the speed of P is $v\,\text{m}\,\text{s}^{-1}$. The particle is at $x = 2$ when $t = 0$. Consider the motion of P in the three cases:

(a) P is projected *away* from O with speed $3\,\text{m}\,\text{s}^{-1}$
(b) P is projected *towards* O with speed $1\,\text{m}\,\text{s}^{-1}$
(c) P is projected *towards* O with speed $9\,\text{m}\,\text{s}^{-1}$.

The equation of motion of the particle is

$$\frac{\mathrm{d}^2 x}{\mathrm{d}t^2} = -4x - 5\frac{\mathrm{d}x}{\mathrm{d}t}$$

at time t seconds. That is:

$$\frac{\mathrm{d}^2 x}{\mathrm{d}t^2} + 5\frac{\mathrm{d}x}{\mathrm{d}t} + 4x = 0$$

Substituting $x = A\mathrm{e}^{\lambda t}$ gives:

$$\lambda^2 + 5\lambda + 4 = 0$$

or:

$$(\lambda + 4)(\lambda + 1) = 0$$

So:

$$\lambda = -1 \quad \text{or} \quad -4$$

Hence:

$$x = A\mathrm{e}^{-4t} + B\mathrm{e}^{-t}$$

(a) You can determine the constants A and B by using the initial conditions.

Since $x = 2$ when $t = 0$,

$$2 = A + B \tag{1}$$

As:

$$x = A\mathrm{e}^{-4t} + B\mathrm{e}^{-t}$$

then:

$$\frac{\mathrm{d}x}{\mathrm{d}t} = -4A\mathrm{e}^{-4t} - B\mathrm{e}^{-t}$$

Since: $\dfrac{\mathrm{d}x}{\mathrm{d}t} = 3$ when $t = 0$,

$$3 = -4A - B \tag{2}$$

Adding equations (1) and (2) gives:

$$5 = -3A$$

so:

$$A = -\tfrac{5}{3} = -1\tfrac{2}{3}$$

From (1):

$$-1\tfrac{2}{3} + B = 2$$

so:

$$B = 2 + 1\tfrac{2}{3} = 3\tfrac{2}{3}$$

The solution for this case is

$$x = -1\tfrac{2}{3}\mathrm{e}^{-4t} + 3\tfrac{2}{3}\mathrm{e}^{-t}$$

In order to sketch x against t note:

(i) $x = 0$ when $-1\frac{2}{3}e^{-4t} + 3\frac{2}{3}e^{-t} = 0$.

or:
$$\tfrac{5}{11} = e^{3t}$$

As $\frac{5}{11}$ is less than 1 and e^{3t} is greater than 1 for $t > 0$, this equation has no real positive solution. Hence **x is never zero for $t \geqslant 0$.**

(ii) $\dfrac{dx}{dt} = 0$ when
$$+\tfrac{20}{3}\, e^{-4t} - \tfrac{11}{3}\, e^{-t} = 0$$

or:
$$\tfrac{20}{11} = e^{3t}$$

As $\frac{20}{11}$ is greater than 1 this equation does have a real positive solution:
$$t_0 = \tfrac{1}{3}\ln\left(\tfrac{20}{11}\right)$$

(iii) Both e^{-4t} and e^{-t} tend to zero as $t \to \infty$. The dependence of x on t in this case is shown in the sketch:

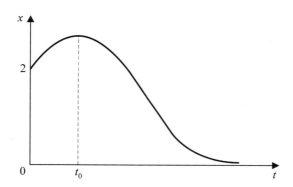

(b) Consider now the general solution:
$$x = A'e^{-4t} + B'e^{-t}$$

Since $x = 2$ when $t = 0$, it follows that:
$$2 = A' + B' \tag{3}$$

As P is now directed *towards* O with speed $1\,\text{m}\,\text{s}^{-1}$,
$$\frac{dx}{dt} = -1 \quad \text{when} \quad t = 0$$

So:
$$-1 = -4A' - B' \tag{4}$$

Adding equations (3) and (4) gives:
$$1 = -3A'$$

so:
$$A' = -\tfrac{1}{3}$$

From (3):
$$-\tfrac{1}{3} + B' = 2$$

so:
$$B' = 2 + \tfrac{1}{3} = 2\tfrac{1}{3}$$

and the solution for this case is

$$x = -\tfrac{1}{3}e^{-4t} + 2\tfrac{1}{3}e^{-t}$$

In order to sketch x against t note:

(i) $x = 0$ when $-\tfrac{1}{3}e^{-4t} + 2\tfrac{1}{3}e^{-t} = 0$

or:
$$\tfrac{1}{7} = e^{3t}$$

As before, since $\tfrac{1}{7}$ is less than 1 this equation has no real positive solution. Hence **x never vanishes for $t \geqslant 0$.**

(ii) $\dfrac{\mathrm{d}x}{\mathrm{d}t} = 0$ when $\tfrac{4}{3}e^{-4t} - \tfrac{7}{3}e^{-t} = 0$

or:
$$\tfrac{4}{7} = e^{3t}$$

As $\tfrac{4}{7}$ is less than 1 this equation has no real positive solution. Hence $\dfrac{\mathrm{d}x}{\mathrm{d}t}$ **never vanishes for $t \geqslant 0$.** The sketch of x against t in this case is:

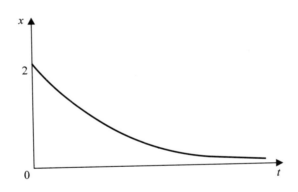

(c) Consider now the general solution:

$$x = A''e^{-4t} + B''e^{-t}$$

Since $x = 2$ when $t = 0$, it follows that:
$$2 = A'' + B'' \tag{5}$$

As P is now directed *towards* O with speed $9\,\mathrm{m\,s^{-1}}$,

$$\frac{\mathrm{d}x}{\mathrm{d}t} = -9 \quad \text{when} \quad t = 0$$

so:
$$-9 = -4A'' - B'' \tag{6}$$

Adding equations (5) and (6) gives:

$$-7 = -3A''$$

so:

$$A'' = \tfrac{7}{3}$$

From (5):

$$\tfrac{7}{3} + B'' = 2$$

so:

$$B'' = -\tfrac{1}{3}$$

and the solution for this case is

$$x = \tfrac{7}{3}e^{-4t} - \tfrac{1}{3}e^{-t}$$

In order to sketch x against t note:

(i) $x = 0$ when $\tfrac{7}{3}e^{-4t} - \tfrac{1}{3}e^{-t} = 0$.

So:

$$7 = e^{3t}$$

or:

$$t_1 = \tfrac{1}{3}\ln 7$$

(ii) $\dfrac{\mathrm{d}x}{\mathrm{d}t} = 0$ when $-\tfrac{28}{3}e^{-4t} + \tfrac{1}{3}e^{-t} = 0$.

So:

$$28 = e^{3t}$$

or:

$$t_2 = \tfrac{1}{3}\ln 28 > t_1$$

The sketch of x against t in this case is

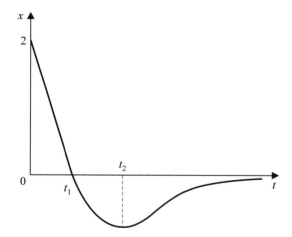

Example 5

A particle P is moving along a horizontal straight line so that at time t seconds its distance x m from a fixed point O of the line satisifes the differential equation:

$$4\frac{\mathrm{d}^2x}{\mathrm{d}t^2} + 12\frac{\mathrm{d}x}{\mathrm{d}t} + 13x = 0$$

(a) Describe a physical situation that could give rise to this equation.

(b) Given that $x = 4$ and $\frac{\mathrm{d}x}{\mathrm{d}t} = 6$ when $t = 0$, obtain the solution of this differential equation.

(c) Hence show that the motion is oscillatory with constant period.

(d) Show also that the amplitudes of successive oscillations decrease in geometric progression.

(a) The given equation can be written:

$$4\frac{\mathrm{d}^2x}{\mathrm{d}t^2} = -13x - 12\frac{\mathrm{d}x}{\mathrm{d}t}$$

or:

$$\frac{\mathrm{d}^2x}{\mathrm{d}t^2} = -\tfrac{13}{4}x - 3\frac{\mathrm{d}x}{\mathrm{d}t}$$

The left-hand side is just the acceleration of the particle P, which can be taken to be of unit mass. Then the term $-\frac{13}{4}x$ is a force whose magnitude is proportional to the distance x metres from a fixed point O of the line of motion. It is directed towards O. The term $-3\frac{\mathrm{d}x}{\mathrm{d}t}$ is a force whose magnitude is proportional to the speed but its direction opposite to the direction of motion. It therefore may be taken as a force resisting the motion.

(b) Substituting $x = A\mathrm{e}^{\lambda t}$ into the differential equation gives the auxiliary equation:

$$4\lambda^2 + 12\lambda + 13 = 0$$

The roots of this equation are

$$\lambda = \frac{-12 \pm \sqrt{[(12)^2 - 4 \times 4 \times 13]}}{2 \times 4}$$

$$= -\tfrac{3}{2} \pm i$$

So the general solution is

$$x = A\mathrm{e}^{-\frac{3}{2}t}\cos t + B\mathrm{e}^{-\frac{3}{2}t}\sin t \qquad (1)$$

Substituting $x = 4$ and $t = 0$ gives:

$$4 = A + 0$$

so:

$$A = 4$$

From (1):

$$\frac{dx}{dt} = A[-\tfrac{3}{2}e^{-\frac{3}{2}t}\cos t + e^{-\frac{3}{2}t}(-\sin t)]$$
$$+ B[-\tfrac{3}{2}e^{-\frac{3}{2}t}\sin t + e^{-\frac{3}{2}t}\cos t]$$

Substituting $\dfrac{dx}{dt} = 6$ and $t = 0$ gives:

$$-\tfrac{3}{2}A + B = 6$$

so:

$$B = \tfrac{3}{2}A + 6 = 12$$

and hence:

$$x = 4e^{-\frac{3}{2}t}\cos t + 12e^{-\frac{3}{2}t}\sin t$$

This may be written as

$$x = e^{-\frac{3}{2}t}[4\cos t + 12\sin t]$$

If

$$4\cos t + 12\sin t = r\cos(t + \alpha)$$
$$= r\cos t\cos\alpha - r\sin t\sin\alpha$$

then:

$$r\cos\alpha = 4 \quad\text{and}\quad r\sin\alpha = -12$$

$$r^2\cos^2\alpha = 16 \quad\text{and}\quad r^2\sin^2\alpha = 144$$

$$r^2(\cos^2\alpha + \sin^2\alpha) = r^2 = 16 + 144 = 160$$

So:

$$r = \sqrt{160} = 4\sqrt{10}$$

$$\tan\alpha = \frac{r\sin\alpha}{r\cos\alpha} = \frac{-12}{4} = -3$$

giving

$$x = 4\sqrt{(10)}e^{-\frac{3}{2}t}\cos(t + \alpha)$$

where $\tan\alpha = -3$.

(c) This solution involves $\cos(t + \alpha)$ which is an oscillating function. It takes the value zero when

$$t + \alpha = (2n + 1)\frac{\pi}{2}$$

where n is an integer. The values of t that satisfy this occur at intervals of π and so the motion is periodic.

(d) $\dfrac{dx}{dt} = 0$ when

$$-\tfrac{3}{2}e^{-\frac{3}{2}t}\cos(t + \alpha) - e^{-\frac{3}{2}t}\sin(t + \alpha) = 0$$

or:
$$\tan(t + \alpha) = -\tfrac{3}{2}$$

$\Rightarrow$
$$t + \alpha = \arctan(-\tfrac{3}{2}) + N\pi$$

where N is an integer.

$$t = \arctan(-\tfrac{3}{2}) - \arctan(-3) + N\pi$$
$$= \beta + N\pi \text{ (say)}$$

Therefore x has stationary values, which are alternately maxima and minima, for values of t given by the equation above. The maxima are given by the even values of N, giving

$$t = \beta + 2n\pi$$

and:
$$\cos^2(t + \alpha) = \frac{1}{\sec^2(t + \alpha)}$$
$$= \frac{1}{1 + \tan^2(t + \alpha)}$$
$$= \frac{1}{1 + \frac{9}{4}} = \frac{4}{13}$$

So:
$$\cos(t + \alpha) = \tfrac{2}{\sqrt{13}}$$

Then successive values of the amplitude are:

$$a_1 = 4\sqrt{10} \times \tfrac{2}{\sqrt{13}} e^{-\frac{3}{2}(\beta + 2\pi)} = (8\sqrt{\tfrac{10}{13}}) e^{-\frac{3\beta}{2} - 3\pi}$$

$$a_2 = 4\sqrt{10} \times \tfrac{2}{\sqrt{13}} e^{-\frac{3}{2}(\beta + 4\pi)} = (8\sqrt{\tfrac{10}{13}}) e^{-\frac{3\beta}{2} - 6\pi}$$

$$a_3 = 4\sqrt{10} \times \tfrac{2}{\sqrt{13}} e^{-\frac{3}{2}(\beta + 6\pi)} = (8\sqrt{\tfrac{10}{13}}) e^{-\frac{3\beta}{2} - 9\pi}$$

and so on.

From this

$$\frac{a_{n+1}}{a_n} = e^{-3\pi}$$

and so the amplitudes decrease in geometric progression.

Example 6

A particle P of mass 2 kg moves along a horizontal straight line under the action of a force directed towards a fixed point O of the line. The force has magnitude $8x$ N when P is at a distance x metres from O. The particle also suffers air resistance which is proportional to its speed and which has magnitude $8v$ N when the speed of P is $v \, \text{m s}^{-1}$. Given that when $t = 0$ the particle is at rest and $x = a$, find the greatest speed of the particle in the ensuing motion.

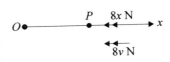

The equation of motion of P is

$$2\frac{d^2x}{dt^2} = -8x - 8\frac{dx}{dt}$$

or:

$$\frac{d^2x}{dt^2} + 4\frac{dx}{dt} + 4x = 0$$

at time t seconds.

Substituting $x = Ae^{\lambda t}$:

$$\lambda^2 + 4\lambda + 4 = 0$$

or:

$$(\lambda + 2)^2 = 0$$

So:

$$\lambda = -2 \quad \text{twice}$$

Hence:

$$x = e^{-2t}(A + Bt) \tag{1}$$

Substituting $x = a$ and $t = 0$ gives:

$$a = A$$

From (1):

$$\frac{dx}{dt} = -2e^{-2t}A + Be^{-2t} - 2Bte^{-2t}$$

Substituting $\dot{x} = 0$ and $t = 0$ gives:

$$0 = -2A + B$$

So:

$$B = 2A = 2a$$

and:

$$x = ae^{-2t}(1 + 2t) \tag{2}$$

The maximum speed of P occurs when $\ddot{x} = 0$.

From (2):

$$\dot{x} = -2ae^{-2t}(1 + 2t) + 2ae^{-2t}$$
$$= -4ate^{-2t}$$

and

$$\ddot{x} = -4ae^{-2t} + 8ate^{-2t}$$

When $\ddot{x} = 0$:

$$-4a + 8at = 0$$

So:

$$t = \tfrac{1}{2}$$

When $t = \tfrac{1}{2}$:

$$\dot{x} = -4a \times \tfrac{1}{2} \times e^{-2 \times \frac{1}{2}} = -2ae^{-1}$$

and so the maximum speed of P is $2ae^{-1}\,\text{m}\,\text{s}^{-1}$.

3.5 Forced harmonic oscillations

In the previous section you saw that, under certain circumstances, a particle subject to two forces – one of which was a restoring force proportional to the particle's displacement and the other of which was a resisting force proportional to its speed – would perform oscillations with a certain period. But what happens if you try to make such a system move in a different way, for example trying to force it to oscillate with a frequency (period) other than its natural one?

Suppose, as before, that the particle is of mass m kg, the restoring force is $m\omega^2 x$ N, where x m is the distance from a fixed point O in the line of motion, and the resistance is mkv N, where v is the speed of the particle. Suppose also that there is an additional applied force of magnitude $mf(t)$ N which varies with time. The equation of motion is now

$$m\ddot{x} = -m\omega^2 x - mk\frac{dx}{dt} + mf(t)$$

or:
$$\ddot{x} + k\dot{x} + \omega^2 x = f(t) \tag{1}$$

The solution of this equation depends on the particular form of the function $f(t)$. However, it can be shown that this solution can always be written as the sum of the general solution of

$$\ddot{x} + k\dot{x} + \omega^2 x = 0$$

called the **complementary equation**, and an additional term. (See chapter 8 of Book P3.)

Suppose one solution of (1) (called a **particular integral**) is

$$x = u$$

Then:
$$\ddot{u} + k\dot{u} + \omega^2 u = f(t)$$

and so equation (1) can be written

$$\ddot{x} + k\dot{x} + \omega^2 x = \ddot{u} + k\dot{u} + \omega^2 u$$

or:
$$(\ddot{x} - \ddot{u}) + k(\dot{x} - \dot{u}) + \omega^2(x - u) = 0$$

That is, $y = x - u$ satisfies

$$\ddot{y} + k\dot{y} + \omega^2 y = 0$$

the complementary equation.

It follows that the general solution of (1) is

$$x = u + y$$

where u is a particular integral of (1) and y is the general solution of the complementary equation, usually called the **complementary function**.

So:

■ $x =$ **(particular integral) + (complementary function)**

The form of the complementary function for the various cases that can arise is given in the previous section. Methods of finding particular integrals are discussed in chapter 8 of Book P3. The following examples indicate the method of solution in the cases:

$$f(t) = A \cos nt + B \sin nt$$
$$f(t) = \alpha + \beta t$$
$$f(t) = k e^{at}$$

Example 7

A particle P of mass m moves on a fixed straight line. At time t, P is a distance x from a fixed point O of the line. The particle is acted on by three forces:

(i) a force $m\omega^2 x$ directed towards O
(ii) a resistance to the motion of magnitude $2m\omega v$, where v is the speed of P
(iii) a force $F = ma \cos \omega t$ acting in the direction of increasing x.

Given that at $t = 0$ the particle is at rest at O, find x as a function of t. Discuss the motion of P.

The equation of motion of P is

$$m\ddot{x} = -m\omega^2 x - 2m\omega \dot{x} + ma \cos \omega t$$

or: $$\ddot{x} + 2\omega \dot{x} + \omega^2 x = a \cos \omega t \qquad (1)$$

The complementary function is the general solution of the complementary equation:

$$\ddot{x} + 2\omega \dot{x} + \omega^2 x = 0$$

Since the auxiliary equation is

$$\lambda^2 + 2\omega \lambda + \omega^2 = 0$$

or: $$(\lambda + \omega)^2 = 0$$

the complementary function is

$$e^{-\omega t}(A + Bt)$$

where A and B are arbitrary constants.

To find the particular integral try

$$x_p = p \cos \omega t + q \sin \omega t \tag{2}$$

where p and q are to be found so that x_p satisfies equation (1).

From (2): $\qquad \dot{x}_p = -p\omega \sin \omega t + q\omega \cos \omega t$

and: $\qquad \ddot{x}_p = -p\omega^2 \cos \omega t - q\omega^2 \sin \omega t$

Substituting x_p, $\dot{x}_p$ and $\ddot{x}_p$ into (1) gives:

$$(-p\omega^2 \cos \omega t - q\omega^2 \sin \omega t) + 2\omega(-p\omega \sin \omega t + q\omega \cos \omega t)$$
$$+ \omega^2(p \cos \omega t + q \sin \omega t) = a \cos \omega t$$

Since this equation must hold for all values of t, you can equate the coefficients of $\sin \omega t$ and $\cos \omega t$ on the two sides of the equation.

$\cos \omega t$: $\qquad -p\omega^2 + 2\omega^2 q + \omega^2 p = a \tag{3a}$

$\sin \omega t$: $\qquad -q\omega^2 - 2\omega^2 p + \omega^2 q = 0 \tag{3b}$

From (3b): $\qquad p = 0$

From (3a): $\qquad q = \dfrac{a}{2\omega^2}$

Hence: $\qquad x_p = \dfrac{a}{2\omega^2} \sin \omega t$

and so the general solution is

$$x = e^{-\omega t}(A + Bt) + \frac{a}{2\omega^2} \sin \omega t \tag{4}$$

Now you can find the values of A and B using the initial conditions $x = 0$ and $\dot{x} = 0$ when $t = 0$.

Since $x = 0$ when $t = 0$

$$0 = A$$

From (4), with $A = 0$:

$$\dot{x} = Be^{-\omega t} - \omega Bte^{-\omega t} + \frac{a\omega}{2\omega^2} \cos \omega t$$

Since $\dot{x} = 0$ when $t = 0$:

$$0 = B + \frac{a}{2\omega}$$

so: $\qquad B = -\dfrac{a}{2\omega}$

and $\qquad x = -\dfrac{at}{2\omega} e^{-\omega t} + \dfrac{a}{2\omega^2} \sin \omega t$

The part of the motion that is represented by $\dfrac{a}{2\omega^2}\sin\omega t$ is an oscillatory motion of constant amplitude $\dfrac{a}{2\omega^2}$ and period $\dfrac{2\pi}{\omega}$ – the period of the forcing term F. It is therefore called the **forced oscillation**. The part $-\dfrac{at}{2\omega}e^{-\omega t}$ tends to zero as $t \to \infty$, as shown earlier. It is called the **transient part** of the motion.

Example 8

A particle P moves along the x-axis so that at time t its displacement from the origin O satisfies the differential equation

$$\frac{d^2x}{dt^2} + 4\frac{dx}{dt} + 13x = 40\cos 3t$$

  (a) Describe a physical situation for which this could be the equation of motion.

  (b) Given that $x = 2$ and $\dfrac{dx}{dt} = 13$ when $t = 0$ find x as a function of t.

  (c) Show that when t is large the motion approximates to simple harmonic motion about O with period $\dfrac{2\pi}{3}$ and amplitude $\sqrt{10}$.

(a) If the given equation is rearranged in the form

$$\ddot{x} = -13x - 4\frac{dx}{dt} + 40\cos 3t$$

then the left-hand side is the acceleration of a particle of unit mass. The first term on the right-hand side represents a restoring force with magnitude proportional to the displacement. The second term represents a resistance to the motion of P proportional to the speed of P. The final term represents an applied periodic force of period $\dfrac{2\pi}{3}$.

(b) The complementary equation is:

$$\ddot{x} + 4\dot{x} + 13x = 0$$

with auxiliary equation

$$\lambda^2 + 4\lambda + 13 = 0$$

The roots of the auxiliary equation are

$$\lambda = \frac{-4 \pm \sqrt{(16 - 4 \times 13)}}{2} = -2 \pm 3i$$

Hence the complementary function is

$$x_c = e^{-2t}(A\cos 3t + B\sin 3t)$$

where A and B are arbitrary constants.

To find a particular solution try

$$x_p = p\cos 3t + q\sin 3t$$

where p and q are to be found so that x_p satisifes the differential equation.

Differentiating x_p with respect to t gives

$$\dot{x}_p = -3p\sin 3t + 3q\cos 3t$$

and

$$\ddot{x}_p = -9p\cos 3t - 9q\sin 3t$$

Substituting x_p, $\dot{x}_p$ and $\ddot{x}_p$ into the differential equation gives:

$$(-9p\cos 3t - 9q\sin 3t) + 4(-3p\sin 3t + 3q\cos 3t)$$
$$+ 13(p\cos 3t + q\sin 3t) = 40\cos 3t$$

Equating coefficients:

$\cos 3t$:	$-9p + 12q + 13p = 40$	(1)
$\sin 3t$:	$-9q - 12p + 13q = 0$	(2)

From (2):
$$-12p + 4q = 0$$
or
$$q = 3p$$

From (1):
$$12q + 4p = 40$$

and substituting for q:

$$12 \times 3p + 4p = 40$$

So:
$$p = 1 \quad \text{and} \quad q = 3$$

and the particular integral is

$$x_p = \cos 3t + 3\sin 3t$$

The general solution is therefore

$$x = x_c + x_p$$
$$= e^{-2t}(A\cos 3t + B\sin 3t) + (\cos 3t + 3\sin 3t)$$

To find A and B you must use the initial conditions.

Since $x = 2$ when $t = 0$,

$$2 = A + 1$$

so:
$$A = 1$$

From the above,

$$\dot{x} = -2e^{-2t}(A\cos 3t + B\sin 3t) + e^{-2t}(-3A\sin 3t + 3B\cos 3t)$$
$$- 3\sin 3t + 9\cos 3t$$

Since $\dot{x} = 13$ when $t = 0$,

$$-2A + 3B + 9 = 13$$

Using $A = 1$ gives

$$3B = 13 - 9 + 2$$

So: $$B = 2$$

and: $$x = e^{-2t}(\cos 3t + 2\sin 3t) + (\cos 3t + 3\sin 3t)$$

(c) When $t \to \infty$ the term $e^{-2t}(\cos 3t + 2\sin 3t)$, which arises from the complementary equation and is therefore sometimes called the **free oscillation**, tends to zero by virtue of the factor e^{-2t}. So for large values of t the motion is given by

$$x_p = \cos 3t + 3\sin 3t$$

You can write this in the form

$$x_p = r\cos(3t + \alpha)$$
$$= r\cos 3t \cos \alpha - r\sin 3t \sin \alpha$$

So: $$r\cos \alpha = 1 \quad \text{and} \quad r\sin \alpha = -3$$
$$r^2 = 10 \quad \text{and} \quad \tan \alpha = -3$$

So: $$x_p = \sqrt{10}\cos(3t + \alpha)$$

This is simple harmonic motion about O of period $\dfrac{2\pi}{3}$ and amplitude $\sqrt{10}$.

Example 9

A particle P of mass m is attached to one end of a light elastic string of natural length l and modulus of elasticity $6mn^2l$, where n is a constant, lying on a horizontal table. The other end of the string is attached to a fixed point O of the horizontal table and P is initially at rest on the table with $OP = l$. A time-dependent force is now applied to P in the direction OP. The magnitude of the force is mn^2le^{-nt} where t is measured from the time the force was initially applied. The motion of the particle is opposed by a resistance of magnitude $5mnv$ where v is the speed of P. Show that when the extension of the string is x,

$$\frac{d^2x}{dt^2} + 5n\frac{dx}{dt} + 6n^2x = n^2le^{-nt}$$

Show that the greatest extension of the string occurs when $t = \dfrac{1}{n} \ln 3$ and find this greatest extension.

Using Hooke's law (Book M2, section 2.3) the tension in the string when the extension is x is $6mn^2l\left(\dfrac{x}{l}\right)$. Therefore for the given situation the equation of motion is

$$m\frac{d^2x}{dt^2} = -6mn^2x - 5mn\frac{dx}{dt} + mn^2le^{-nt}$$

or:

$$\frac{d^2x}{dt^2} + 5n\frac{dx}{dt} + 6n^2x = n^2le^{-nt} \tag{1}$$

The complementary equation is

$$\ddot{x} + 5n\dot{x} + 6n^2x = 0$$

with auxiliary equation

$$\lambda^2 + 5n\lambda + 6n^2 = 0$$

This equation factorises to give:

$$(\lambda + 3n)(\lambda + 2n) = 0$$

and so has roots $\lambda = -3n$ and $\lambda = -2n$.

Hence the complementary function is

$$x_c = Ae^{-3nt} + Be^{-2nt}$$

where A and B are arbitrary constants.

To find a particular solution try

$$x_p = Ce^{-nt}$$

where C is a constant to be found.

Then:

$$\dot{x}_p = -Cne^{-nt}$$

and:

$$\ddot{x}_p = Cn^2e^{-nt}$$

Substituting into equation (1) gives:

$$C(n^2 - 5n^2 + 6n^2)e^{-nt} = n^2le^{-nt}$$

Since e^{-nt} is not zero,

$$2n^2C = n^2l$$

and

$$C = \frac{l}{2}$$

so that

$$x_p = \frac{l}{2}e^{-nt}$$

Hence the general solution of (1) is

$$x = Ae^{-3nt} + Be^{-2nt} + \tfrac{1}{2}le^{-nt} \qquad (2)$$

You can find the constants A and B by using the initial conditions $x = 0$ and $\dot{x} = 0$ when $t = 0$.

Since $x = 0$ when $t = 0$,

$$0 = A + B + \tfrac{1}{2}l \qquad (3)$$

From (2): $\qquad \dot{x} = -3nAe^{-3nt} - 2nBe^{-2nt} - \tfrac{1}{2}lne^{-nt}$

Subsituting $\dot{x} = 0$ when $t = 0$ gives:

$$0 = -3nA - 2nB - \tfrac{1}{2}ln \qquad (4)$$

Solving equations (3) and (4) simultaneously gives:

$$A = \tfrac{1}{2}l \quad \text{and} \quad B = -l$$

so that:

$$x = \tfrac{1}{2}le^{-3nt} - le^{-2nt} + \tfrac{1}{2}le^{-nt} \qquad (5)$$

The greatest extension of the string occurs when $\dot{x} = 0$. That is:

$$-\tfrac{3}{2}nle^{-3nt} + 2nle^{-2nt} - \tfrac{1}{2}lne^{-nt} = 0$$

or:

$$\left(\frac{-nl}{2}\right)e^{-3nt}[3 - 4e^{nt} + e^{2nt}] = 0$$

so that:

$$e^{2nt} - 4e^{nt} + 3 = 0$$

This factorises to give:

$$(e^{nt} - 3)(e^{nt} - 1) = 0$$

so that:

$$e^{nt} = 1 \quad \text{or} \quad 3$$

that is:

$$t = 0 \quad \text{or} \quad \frac{1}{n}\ln 3$$

When $t = 0$, $x = 0$ and when $t = \dfrac{1}{n}\ln 3$ the extension of the string is a maximum.

When $t = \dfrac{1}{n} \ln 3$, $e^{-nt} = \frac{1}{3}$ and so:

$$x = \tfrac{1}{2} l (\tfrac{1}{3})^3 - l(\tfrac{1}{3})^2 + \tfrac{1}{2} l(\tfrac{1}{3})$$

$$= l[\tfrac{1}{54} - \tfrac{1}{9} + \tfrac{1}{6}]$$

$$= \frac{l}{54}[1 - 6 + 9]$$

$$= \tfrac{2}{27} l$$

So the greatest extension is $\tfrac{2}{27} l$.

Example 10

A light string AB having natural length l and modulus of elasticity $3lmn^2$ lies straight and at its natural length at rest on a horizontal table. A particle of mass m is attached to the end A. The end B is then moved in a straight line in the direction AB with constant acceleration f. The resulting motion of the particle is resisted by a force of magnitude $4mnv$ where v is the speed of the particle. If x is the extension of the string at time t show that

$$\frac{\mathrm{d}^2 x}{\mathrm{d}t^2} + 4n \frac{\mathrm{d}x}{\mathrm{d}t} + 3n^2 x = 4nft + f$$

Find x as a function of t.

Suppose the situation at time t, relative to the initial position, is as shown:

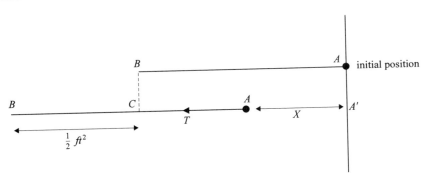

Since B moves in the direction AB with constant acceleration f, then:

$$CB = \tfrac{1}{2} ft^2$$

If A has moved a distance X from its original position A' then the length of the string is

$$l + \tfrac{1}{2} ft^2 - X$$

and so the extension x of the string is

$$x = (l + \tfrac{1}{2}ft^2 - X) - l = \tfrac{1}{2}ft^2 - X$$

and the speed of the particle A is

$$\frac{dX}{dt} = \frac{d}{dt}(\tfrac{1}{2}ft^2 - x) = ft - \frac{dx}{dt}$$

From the given information the equation of motion of the particle in the direction AB is

$$m\frac{d^2 X}{dt^2} = (\text{tension in string}) - (\text{resisting force})$$

Now:

$$\frac{d^2 X}{dt^2} = f - \frac{d^2 x}{dt^2}$$

$$\text{tension in string} = \frac{3lmn^2}{l} x$$

$$\text{resisting force} = 4mnv$$

$$= 4mn\frac{dX}{dt}$$

$$= 4mn\left[ft - \frac{dx}{dt}\right]$$

So:

$$m\left(f - \frac{d^2 x}{dt^2}\right) = 3mn^2 x - 4mn\left(ft - \frac{dx}{dt}\right)$$

or:

$$\frac{d^2 x}{dt^2} + 4n\frac{dx}{dt} + 3n^2 x = 4nft + f \tag{1}$$

The complementary equation is

$$\ddot{x} + 4n\dot{x} + 3n^2 x = 0$$

with auxiliary equation

$$\lambda^2 + 4n\lambda + 3n^2 = 0$$

This equation factorises to give:

$$(\lambda + 3n)(\lambda + n) = 0$$

and so has roots $\lambda = -3n$ and $\lambda = -n$.

Hence the complementary function is

$$x_c = Ae^{-3nt} + Be^{-nt}$$

where A and B are arbitrary constants.

To find a particular solution try:

$$x_p = at + b$$

where a and b are constants to be determined. Using $\dot{x}_p = a$ and $\ddot{x}_p = 0$ and substituting into equation (1) gives:

$$0 + 4na + 3n^2(at + b) = 4nft + f$$

If you equate the terms involving t on the two sides of this equation, you get:

$$3n^2 at = 4nft$$

so:

$$a = \frac{4f}{3n}$$

From the terms not involving t:

$$4na + 3n^2 b = f$$

Substituting the value of a found above gives:

$$\frac{16f}{3} + 3n^2 b = f$$

$\Rightarrow$

$$b = \frac{1}{3n^2}\left(f - \frac{16f}{3}\right) = -\frac{13f}{9n^2}$$

So:

$$x_p = \left(\frac{4f}{3n}\right)t - \frac{13f}{9n^2}$$

and the general solution is

$$x = Ae^{-3nt} + Be^{-nt} + \left(\frac{4f}{3n}\right)t - \frac{13f}{9n^2}$$

Using the initial conditions $x = 0$ and $\dot{x} = 0$ when $t = 0$ gives:

$x = 0$:

$$A + B - \frac{13f}{9n^2} = 0$$

$\dot{x} = 0$:

$$-3nA - nB + \frac{4f}{3n} = 0$$

Solving these equations simultaneously for A and B gives:

$$A = -\frac{f}{18n^2} \qquad B = \frac{3f}{2n^2}$$

and so:

$$x = \left(-\frac{f}{18n^2}\right)e^{-3nt} + \left(\frac{3f}{2n^2}\right)e^{-nt} + \left(\frac{4f}{3n}\right)t - \frac{13f}{9n^2}$$

Exercise 3B

In questions 1–3 the differential equation is the equation of motion of a particle P moving in a straight line under the action of two forces:

(i) a restoring force directed towards a fixed point O of the line with magnitude proportional to the distance x m of P from O,

(ii) a resistance to its motion with magnitude proportional to its speed.

1 $\ddot{x} + 2\dot{x} + 2x = 0$ with $x = 1$ and $\dot{x} = 0$ when $t = 0$. Calculate x when $t = \dfrac{\pi}{2}$ and describe the motion.

2 $\ddot{x} + 2\dot{x} + x = 0$ with $x = 4$ and $\dot{x} = 0$ when $t = 0$. Find x as a function of t and show that x never vanishes for $t \geqslant 0$. Find the speed of P when $t = 2$.

3 $\ddot{x} + 2\dot{x} + 5x = 0$ with $x = 2$ and $\dot{x} = 0$ when $t = 0$. Find x as a function of t and show that the smallest non-zero value of t for which $\dot{x}$ is zero is $t = \dfrac{\pi}{2}$.

4 A particle P of mass 1 kg moves in a horizontal straight line under the action of a force directed towards a fixed point O of the line. The force varies as the distance of the particle from O and is equal to $2x$ N when P is at a distance x metres from O. The particle is also subject to a resisting force whose magnitude is proportional to its speed and which is equal to $3v$ N when the speed of P is v m s^{-1}. Given that P starts from rest when $x = 1$ and $t = 0$, find x as a function of t and obtain the value of t when $x = \frac{1}{10}$.

5 A particle P moves along a straight line so that its displacement, x metres, from a fixed point O of the line at time t seconds is given by

$$x = 3e^{-t} \cos 2t$$

(a) Show that the particle performs oscillations about O with constant period.

(b) Show that the amplitude of the motion decreases in geometric progression.

(c) Show that $\ddot{x} + 2\dot{x} + 5x = 0$

6 A particle of mass m moves in a straight line. At time t its displacement from a fixed point O of the line is x. Explain the

nature of the forces acting on the particle, given that the equation of motion can be written as:

$$\frac{d^2x}{dt^2} + 2k\frac{dx}{dt} + 10k^2x = 0$$

where k is a positive constant.
Given that $x = 0$ and $\frac{dx}{dt} = u$ when $t = 0$,

(a) find x as a function of t

(b) show that when x is next zero

$$\frac{dx}{dt} = -ue^{-\pi/3}$$

7   A simple pendulum in a vacuum performs small oscillations, of period $\frac{\pi}{2}$ seconds, about its equilibrium position. The pendulum is placed in a fluid and now performs small oscillations under gravity in the fluid, which offers resistance to the motion of the bob. The resistance is of magnitude $2mkv$, where m is the mass and v the speed of the bob; k is a constant whose value depends on the nature of the fluid. Show that θ, the angular displacement of the pendulum from the vertical, satisfies the differential equation

$$\frac{d^2\theta}{dt^2} + 2k\frac{d\theta}{dt} + 16\theta = 0$$

Given that $k = 2$, show that

$$\theta = ae^{-2t}\sin(2\sqrt{3}t)$$

gives a possible solution, where a is a small arbitrary constant. Sketch a graph of θ against t.

8   A particle P of mass m is attached to one end of an elastic string of natural length l and modulus of elasticity mg. The other end of the string is attached to a fixed point O and the system hangs freely under gravity. The particle is pulled down so that the string is vertical and of length $3l$. The particle is now released from rest and moves in a medium which exerts a resistance of magnitude $\left(\frac{3g}{l}\right)^{\frac{1}{2}}mv$, where v is the speed of P. Show that the

extension x of the string at time t satisfies the differential equation

$$l\frac{d^2x}{dt^2} + (3gl)^{\frac{1}{2}}\frac{dx}{dt} + g(x - l) = 0$$

Show that the string does not become slack in the subsequent motion and that the particle is next at rest when its depth below O is

$$l(2 - e^{-\sqrt{3}\pi})$$

9 A particle P is attached to one end of a spring the other end of which oscillates. The displacement x of P from a fixed reference point at time t satisfies the differential equation

$$\frac{d^2x}{dt^2} + 4x = \lambda \sin t$$

where λ is a constant. Given that $x = 0$ and $\dfrac{dx}{dt} = \dfrac{2\lambda}{3}$ when $t = 0$, find x as a function of t.

10 A light spring AB, having natural length a and modulus of elasticity $3amn^2$, lies straight and at its natural length at rest on a horizontal table. A particle of mass m is attached to the end A. The end B is then moved in a straight line in the direction AB with constant speed V. The resulting motion of the particle is resisted by a force of magnitude $4mnv$ where v is the speed of the particle. If x is the extension of the spring at time t, show that

$$\frac{d^2x}{dt^2} + 4n\frac{dx}{dt} + 3n^2x = 4nV$$

Obtain x in terms of t.

11 A particle of mass m lies at rest on a horizontal table and is attached to one end of a light spring which, when stretched, exerts a tension of magnitude $m\omega^2 \times$ (extension of the spring), where ω is constant. The other end of the spring is now moved with constant speed u along the table in a direction away from the particle. The resistance to the motion of the particle provided by the table is of magnitude $mk \times$ (the speed of the particle), where k is constant.

(a) Obtain the differential equation satisfied by x, the extension of the spring after time t.

(b) Given that $k = 2\omega$ show that

$$x = \frac{u}{\omega}[2 - (2 + \omega t)e^{-\omega t}]$$

3.6 Motion of a particle with varying mass

In all the problems considered thus far in this book and the earlier books M1 and M2, the mass of the body or particle involved has been assumed to be constant. However, there are some problems where the mass of the body changes; for example, a rocket, whose mass becomes less as its motors burn up fuel; or a raindrop, whose mass becomes greater as it passes through a cloud. Such problems are usually called 'variable mass' problems but in fact the mass in the problem is being redistributed rather than changing.

In problems of this kind, rather than write down the equations of motion of the system, we usually use the **impulse–momentum principle**. The system will be assumed to consist of the body in motion together with any matter that is ejected in a small interval of time δt or any matter that is absorbed in this time interval. At the beginning of this interval the various parts of the system will have their separate motions; at the end of the interval each part will normally have a different motion.

- **The impulse–momentum principle states: Change of linear momentum of the whole system in time interval δt = impulse of external forces acting on whole system in time interval δt.**

Suppose the body picks up material of mass δm in the interval and that its speed increases by δv. The quantity $\delta m \cdot \delta v$ tends to zero more rapidly than δm or δv do as $\delta t \to 0$ and so such products may be neglected in writing down the impulse–momentum equation. You can then set up a differential equation by dividing by δt and taking the limit as $\delta t \to 0$.

In each case proceed from first principles and derive the differential equation from scratch. Do not try to quote standard results. The method is illustrated in the following examples.

Example 11

A body has mass m and speed v at time t and picks up matter when falling under constant gravity. Obtain the differential equation satisifed by m

    (a) when the matter being picked up is not moving
    (b) when the matter being picked up has speed u.

(a) Consider the system as the body of mass m and the material of mass δm.

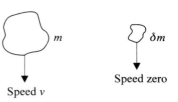

The initial momentum is then

$$mv + \delta m \times 0 = mv$$

At the end of the interval the body and material have coalesced to form a body of mass $(m + \delta m)$ moving with a speed $(v + \delta v)$. The final momentum is then

$$(m + \delta m)(v + \delta v)$$

The external force acting on the system is the total weight $mg + (\delta m)g$.

By the impulse–momentum principle:

Change in momentum = impulse of external force   (1)
$$(m + \delta m)(v + \delta v) - mv = (m + \delta m)g\delta t$$

so that: $mv + m\delta v + v\delta m + \delta m \cdot \delta v - mv = mg\delta t + g\delta m \cdot \delta t$

Neglecting the term $\delta m \cdot \delta v$ and dividing by δt gives:

$$mg + g\delta m = m\frac{\delta v}{\delta t} + v\frac{\delta m}{\delta t}$$

Taking the limit as $\delta t \to 0$ and using the fact that $\delta m \to 0$ gives:

$$mg = m\frac{dv}{dt} + v\frac{dm}{dt} = \frac{d}{dt}(mv) \qquad (2)$$

(b) If the matter picked up was moving with speed u rather than being at rest, the initial momentum would be $mv + \delta m \cdot u$ and equation (1) is then modified to:

$$(m + \delta m)(v + \delta v) - (mv + \delta m u) = (m + \delta m)g\delta t$$

This leads to the differential equation

$$mg = m\frac{dv}{dt} + v\frac{dm}{dt} - u\frac{dm}{dt} \qquad (3)$$

Notice that equation (2) expresses Newton's second law in the form

(rate of change of downward momentum) = (downward force)

However, equation (3) shows that the result must be modified when the additional mass is not picked up from rest.

Example 12

A body moves vertically upwards under gravity. At time t its mass is m and its speed is v. The body ejects material at a rate of k units of mass per second vertically downwards with a speed u relative to the body. Obtain the differential equation satisfied by m.

At the start of the interval the body has mass m and speed v. At the end of the time interval δt it has mass $(m + \delta m)$. A mass

$$-\delta m = k \delta t$$

has been ejected. The speed is now $(v + \delta v)$. The ejected mass has a speed $(v - u)$ at the start of the interval and $(v + \delta v - u)$ at the end of the interval. The upward momentum of the ejected mass lies between $-\delta m(v - u)$ and $-\delta m(v + \delta v - u)$ and since we neglect terms in $\delta m \cdot \delta v$ this will be taken as $-\delta m(v - u)$. Finally, the external force acting on the whole system is mg. Using the impulse–momentum principle gives:

$$[(m + \delta m)(v + \delta v) + (-\delta m)(v - u)] - mv = -mg\delta t$$

Neglecting the term in $\delta m \cdot \delta v$ this reduces to

$$m\delta v + u\delta m = -mg\delta t$$

Dividing by δt and taking the limit as $\delta t \to 0$ gives:

$$m\frac{dv}{dt} + u\frac{dm}{dt} = -mg$$

But:

$$\frac{dm}{dt} = -k$$

So:

$$m\frac{dv}{dt} - ku = -mg$$

Example 13

A spherical hailstone, falling under gravity in still air, increases its radius by condensation according to the law $\dfrac{dr}{dt} = kr$, where k is constant. Neglecting air resistance, show that the hailstone approaches the limiting speed $\left(\dfrac{g}{3k}\right)$.

By the impulse–momentum principle:

$$\text{change in momentum} = \text{impulse of external force}$$

Since the added material is picked up from rest this gives:

$$(m + \delta m)(v + \delta v) - mv = (m + \delta m)g\delta t$$

Neglecting the term $\delta m \cdot \delta v$, dividing by δt and taking the limit as $\delta t \to 0$ gives:

$$m\frac{dv}{dt} + v\frac{dm}{dt} = mg$$

As the hailstone is spherical in this case,

$$m = \tfrac{4}{3}\pi r^3 \rho$$

where ρ is the density of the ice. The equation becomes:

$$\tfrac{4}{3}\pi r^3 \rho \frac{dv}{dt} + v\frac{d}{dt}(\tfrac{4}{3}\pi r^3 \rho) = \tfrac{4}{3}\pi r^3 \rho g$$

or:

$$r^3 \frac{dv}{dt} + v\frac{d}{dt}(r^3) = r^3 g$$

$$r^3 \frac{dv}{dt} + 3vr^2 \frac{dr}{dt} = r^3 g$$

Using $\dfrac{dr}{dt} = kr$ gives:

$$r^3 \frac{dv}{dt} + 3kr^3 v = r^3 g$$

or:

$$\frac{dv}{dt} = g - 3kv$$

You can find the limiting speed by setting $\dfrac{dv}{dt} = 0$.

So:

$$v\,(\text{limiting}) = \left(\frac{g}{3k}\right)$$

Exercise 3C

1 A rocket has initial total mass M. It propels itself by ejecting mass at a constant rate k per unit time with speed u relative to the rocket. The rocket is launched from rest vertically upwards. Show that its speed after time t is

$$-u\ln\left(1 - \frac{kt}{M}\right) - gt$$

provided that $ku > Mg$. Explain why this condition is required.

2 A spherical raindrop of radius a falls from rest under gravity. It falls through a stationary cloud so that, because of condensation, its radius increases with time at a constant rate k. Find the distance fallen by the raindrop after time t.

3 A small body, of mass m_0, is projected vertically upwards in a cloud. Its initial speed is $(2gk)^{\frac{1}{2}}$. During its motion the body picks up moisture from the stationary cloud. Its mass at height x above the point of projection is $m_0(1 + \alpha x)$, where α is a positive constant. Show that the greatest height h satisfies the equation

$$(1 + \alpha h)^3 = (1 + 3k\alpha)$$

4 A body consists of equal masses M of inflammable and non-inflammable material. The body descends freely under gravity from rest. The combustible part burns at a constant rate of kM per second, where k is a constant. The burning material is ejected vertically upwards with constant speed u relative to the body, and air resistance may be neglected. Show, using momentum considerations, that

$$\frac{d}{dt}[(2 - kt)v] = k(u - v) + g(2 - kt)$$

where v is the speed of the body at time t. Hence show that the body descends a distance

$$\frac{g}{2k^2} + \frac{u}{k}(1 - \ln 2)$$

before all the inflammable material is burnt.

5 A rocket is fired vertically upwards with initial speed V and is propelled by ejecting material downwards at a constant rate and with a constant speed u relative to the rocket. After a time T the propellant material is exhausted and the rocket still rising. Neglecting air resistance, show that the maximum height h attained is given by:

$$2gh = (u\ln \lambda)^2 - 2Vu\ln \lambda + V^2 + 2guT[1 + (1 - \lambda)^{-1}\ln \lambda]$$

where λ is the ratio of the mass of the rocket alone to the total initial mass of the rocket and propellant.

SUMMARY OF KEY POINTS

1 For a particle P travelling in a straight line, which at time t seconds has a displacement x metres from a fixed point O of the line and a velocity of $v\,\text{m}\,\text{s}^{-1}$ the acceleration $a\,\text{m}\,\text{s}^{-2}$ is given by

$$a = \frac{\mathrm{d}v}{\mathrm{d}t}$$

or:

$$a = v\frac{\mathrm{d}v}{\mathrm{d}x} = \frac{\mathrm{d}}{\mathrm{d}x}\left(\tfrac{1}{2}v^2\right)$$

2 Displacements must always be measured from a *fixed* point.

3 When resistance, proportional to the speed, is taken into account the S.H.M. equation becomes

$$\ddot{x} + k\dot{x} + \omega^2 x = 0$$

The form of the solution depends on the nature of the solution of the corresponding auxiliary equation

$$\lambda^2 + k\lambda + \omega^2 = 0$$

that is, whether the roots are real and distinct, equal or complex.

4 When there is an additional time-dependent force $m\mathrm{f}(t)$ the damped harmonic equation becomes

$$\ddot{x} + k\dot{x} + \omega^2 x = \mathrm{f}(t)$$

The general solution of this equation is

$$x = x_\mathrm{c} \text{ (complementary function)}$$
$$+ x_\mathrm{p}\text{(particular integral)}$$

5 To solve problems involving changing mass apply the impulse–momentum principle:

change of linear momentum of the whole system in time interval δt = impulse of external forces acting on whole system in time interval δt

Elastic collisions in two dimensions

4

Chapter 5 of Book M2 was concerned with 'collisions'. However, the treatment there was restricted to one-dimensional problems such as the direct impact of two particles moving in the same straight line and normal impact of a particle with a fixed surface. Such an impact is unusual in real situations. So in this chapter we shall consider the generalisation of that work to elastic collisions in two-dimensional situations.

Assume that the elastic bodies involved in the collisions are **smooth**. This means that the mutual reaction acts along **the common normal at the point of impact**. For example, when two elastic spheres collide the mutual reaction acts along **the line of centres**.

By the impulse–momentum principle there is **no change in the momentum** of the bodies involved in the collision **perpendicular** to this common normal and hence:

■ **the components of the velocities of the bodies involved in the collision perpendicular to the common normal are unchanged.**

The components of the velocities of the bodies involved in the collision **parallel to this common normal** can be found in the same manner as for direct impact. That is:

(i) total momentum in this direction before impact
   = total momentum in this direction after impact

(ii) $\dfrac{\text{speed of separation in this direction}}{\text{speed of approach in this direction}} = e$

where e is the coefficient of restitution between the bodies (Newton's law of restitution).

So it follows that, if you have an elastic collision, you must deal with the motions along the common normal and perpendicular to it separately. In the particular case of two elastic spheres colliding, this means that the motions along and perpendicular to the line of centres must be dealt with separately. You will see this clearly in the next two sections when we consider the cases of oblique impact of a smooth sphere with a fixed smooth surface and oblique impact of two smooth spheres.

4.1 Impact of a smooth sphere with a fixed smooth plane

Consider a smooth sphere that strikes a fixed smooth plane *obliquely*, that is, not along the normal to the plane. Suppose that the sphere has speed u and that its direction of motion makes an angle α with the fixed plane. Since the sphere is smooth and the plane is smooth the mutual reaction between the sphere and the plane will act along the normal to the plane at the point of impact. So we can consider the motions parallel to the plane and perpendicular to the plane separately. Just before impact we have:

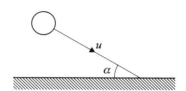

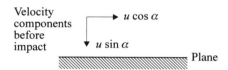

Suppose that after the impact the sphere has speed v and that its direction of motion makes an angle β with the fixed plane:

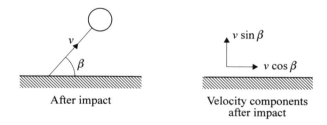

After impact   Velocity components
                                after impact

(i) Perpendicular to the common normal, that is, parallel to the plane, there is no change in the component of the velocity so that

$$u \cos \alpha = v \cos \beta \qquad (1)$$

(ii) Perpendicular to the plane:

$$\frac{\text{component of velocity in this direction after collision}}{\text{component of velocity in this direction before collision}} = e$$

or

(component of velocity after collision) $= e$(component of velocity before collision)

$$v \sin \beta = eu \sin \alpha$$

$$(2)$$

You can use the solutions of equations (1) and (2) to calculate the changes in the speed and direction of motion of the sphere and also the change in momentum and loss of kinetic energy as a result of the impact.

Example 1

A small smooth sphere of mass 2 kg is projected along a smooth horizontal table towards a fixed smooth vertical wall. Before impact with the wall it has a speed of $12\,\mathrm{m\,s^{-1}}$ and its direction of motion makes an angle of 30° with the wall. Given that the coefficient of restitution between the sphere and the wall is $\frac{1}{4}$

(a) calculate the velocity of the sphere after the impact.
(b) Find also the magnitude of the impulse exerted by the wall on the sphere.

(a) The situation *before impact* is:

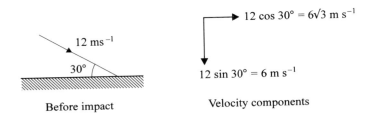

Before impact   Velocity components

Suppose that the final speed is $v\,\mathrm{m\,s^{-1}}$ and the direction of motion makes an angle β with the wall. The situation *after impact* is:

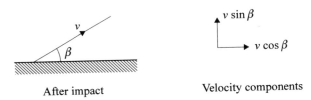

After impact   Velocity components

(i) *Parallel to the wall*
   No change in velocity component, so:

$$6\sqrt{3} = v\cos\beta \qquad (1)$$

(ii) *Perpendicular to the wall*
   Newton's law of restitution gives:

$$v\sin\beta = \tfrac{1}{4} \times 6 = 1\tfrac{1}{2} \qquad (2)$$

Squaring and adding equations (1) and (2) gives:

$$v^2 \sin^2 \beta + v^2 \cos^2 \beta = v^2 = (6\sqrt{3})^2 + (1\tfrac{1}{2})^2$$
$$= 110\tfrac{1}{4}$$

So:
$$v = 10\tfrac{1}{2}$$

Dividing (2) by (1) gives:

$$\frac{v \sin \beta}{v \cos \beta} = \tan \beta = \frac{1\tfrac{1}{2}}{6\sqrt{3}} = \frac{\sqrt{3}}{12}$$

So:
$$\beta = 8.21°$$

So the sphere has speed $10\tfrac{1}{2}\,\text{m s}^{-1}$ and the direction of motion makes an angle of 8.21° with the wall.

(b) Now consider the motion of the sphere perpendicular to the wall. Impulse exerted by the wall on the sphere

$$= \text{change in momentum of the sphere}$$
$$= 2v \sin \beta + 2(12 \sin 30°)$$
$$= 2(1\tfrac{1}{2}) + 2(6) = 15$$

So the magnitude of the impulse exerted by the wall on the sphere is 15 Ns.

Example 2

A small smooth sphere is moving in the xy-plane and collides with a smooth fixed vertical wall which contains the y-axis. The velocity of the sphere just before impact is $(4\mathbf{j} - 5\mathbf{i})\,\text{m s}^{-1}$. Given that the coefficient of restitution between the sphere and the wall is $\tfrac{1}{5}$,

   (a) find the velocity of the sphere immediately after impact.
   (b) Given further that the sphere is of mass 3 kg, find the loss of kinetic energy as a result of the impact.

This diagram summarises the given information:

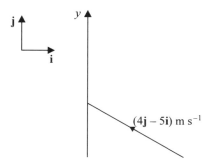

Let the velocity after the impact be $(u\mathbf{i} + v\mathbf{j})\,\mathrm{m\,s^{-1}}$. The components of velocity are then:

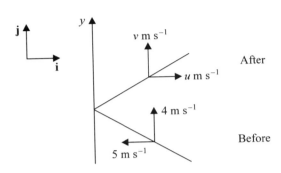

(i) *Parallel to the wall*
No change of velocity component $\Rightarrow v = 4$

(ii) *Perpendicular to the wall*
Newton's law of resitution $\Rightarrow u = \frac{1}{5} \times 5 = 1$

So the velocity of the sphere after the impact is $(\mathbf{i} + 4\mathbf{j})\,\mathrm{m\,s^{-1}}$.

(b) The kinetic energy of the sphere before impact is

$$\tfrac{1}{2} \times 3 \times (4^2 + 5^2) = \tfrac{3}{2} \times 41$$

The kinetic energy of the sphere after impact is

$$\tfrac{1}{2} \times 3 \times (1^2 + 4^2) = \tfrac{3}{2} \times 17$$

$$\text{Loss of K.E.} = \tfrac{3}{2}(41 - 17) = 36\,\mathrm{J}$$

Example 3

A smooth sphere strikes a smooth fixed wall with speed $u\,\mathrm{m\,s^{-1}}$ at an angle of $30°$ to the wall. It rebounds with speed $16\,\mathrm{m\,s^{-1}}$ at an angle of β to the wall. Given that the coefficient of restitution between the sphere and the wall is $\frac{1}{2}$, find u and β.
The given information is summarised in the figure:

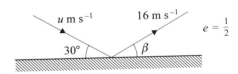

(i) *Parallel to the wall*

$$u \cos 30° = 16 \cos \beta$$

$$\frac{u\sqrt{3}}{2} = 16 \cos \beta \tag{1}$$

(ii) *Perpendicular to the wall*
Newton's law of restitution gives:

$$16 \sin \beta = \tfrac{1}{2}u \sin 30° = \tfrac{1}{2}u \times \tfrac{1}{2} = \tfrac{1}{4}u \tag{2}$$

Squaring and adding equations (1) and (2) gives:

$$(16)^2 \cos^2 \beta + (16)^2 \sin^2 \beta = \tfrac{3}{4}u^2 + \tfrac{1}{16}u^2$$

or:

$$(16)^2 = u^2(\tfrac{3}{4} + \tfrac{1}{16}) = \tfrac{13}{16}u^2$$

$\Rightarrow$

$$u^2 = \frac{(16)^2 \times 16}{13}$$

and $u = 17.8$

Dividing (2) by (1) gives:

$$\frac{16 \sin \beta}{16 \cos \beta} = \frac{\tfrac{1}{4}u}{u\frac{\sqrt{3}}{2}} = \frac{2}{4\sqrt{3}}$$

So:

$$\tan \beta = \frac{1}{2\sqrt{3}}$$

$\Rightarrow$

$$\beta = 16.1°$$

Example 4

A smooth sphere strikes a smooth fixed wall with speed $u \, \text{m s}^{-1}$ at an angle of 45° to the wall. It rebounds with speed $v \, \text{m s}^{-1}$ at an angle of 60° to the wall. Find the coefficient of restitution between the sphere and the wall.

The given information can be summarised in a diagram:

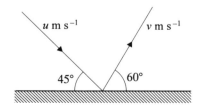

(i) *Parallel to the wall*

$$u\cos 45° = v\cos 60°$$

or
$$u\frac{\sqrt{2}}{2} = v\frac{1}{2} \qquad (1)$$

(ii) *Perpendicular to the wall*
Newton's law of restitution gives:

$$v\sin 60° = eu\sin 45°$$

or
$$v\frac{\sqrt{3}}{2} = eu\frac{\sqrt{2}}{2} \qquad (2)$$

Dividing (2) by (1) eliminates both u and v and gives:

$$e = \sqrt{3}$$

Exercise 4A

1 A smooth billiard ball is projected along a smooth horizontal table towards a fixed smooth vertical cushion. Before impact with the cushion it has a speed of $20\,\mathrm{m\,s^{-1}}$ and its direction of motion makes an angle of $30°$ with the cushion. Given that the coefficient of restitution between the billiard ball and the cushion is $\frac{2}{5}$, find the magnitude and direction of the velocity of the billiard ball after impact.

2 A small smooth sphere is projected along a smooth horizontal table towards a fixed smooth vertical wall. Before impact with the wall it has a speed of $8\,\mathrm{m\,s^{-1}}$ and its direction of motion makes an angle of $40°$ with the wall. Given that the coefficient of restitution between the sphere and the wall is $\frac{3}{10}$, find the magnitude and direction of the velocity of the sphere after impact.

3 A small smooth sphere of mass $2\,\mathrm{kg}$ is moving in the xy-plane and collides with a smooth fixed vertical wall which contains the y-axis. The velocity of the sphere just before impact is $(2\mathbf{j} - 6\mathbf{i})\,\mathrm{m\,s^{-1}}$. The coefficient of restitution between the sphere and the wall is $\frac{1}{2}$. Find
   (a) the velocity of the sphere after impact
   (b) the loss of kinetic energy due to the impact

(c) the impulse exerted by the wall on the sphere.

4 A small smooth sphere of mass 1.5 kg is moving in the xy-plane and collides with a smooth fixed vertical wall which contains the x-axis. The velocity of the sphere just before impact is $(2\mathbf{i} - 9\mathbf{j})\,\mathrm{m\,s^{-1}}$. The coefficient of restitution between the sphere and the wall is $\frac{1}{3}$. Find

(a) the velocity of the sphere after impact

(b) the impulse exerted by the wall on the sphere.

5 A smooth billiard ball strikes a smooth cushion with speed $u\,\mathrm{m\,s^{-1}}$ at an angle of $60°$ to the cushion. Given that the coefficient of restitution between the ball and the cushion is $\frac{1}{3}$, show that the ball rebounds at right angles to its original direction of motion.

6 A small smooth spherical ball of mass m falls vertically and strikes a fixed smooth inclined plane with speed u.

(a) Explain why the component of the velocity of the ball parallel to the plane is not affected by the impact.

The plane is inclined at $\alpha°$ to the horizontal, $\alpha < 45$. The ball rebounds horizontally.

(b) Show that $e = \tan^2 \alpha°$.

(c) Show that a fraction $(1 - e)$ of the kinetic energy is lost during the impact.

(d) Show also that the magnitude of the impulse exerted on the sphere by the plane is $mu \sec \alpha°$.

7 A smooth snooker ball strikes a smooth cushion when moving in a direction inclined at $60°$ to the cushion. The ball rebounds at an angle of $45°$ to the cushion. Show that one half of the kinetic energy of the ball is lost in the impact.

8 Two smooth vertical walls stand on a smooth horizontal floor and intersect at an acute angle θ. A small smooth particle is projected along the floor at right angles to one of the walls and away from it. After one impact with each wall the particle is moving parallel to the first wall it struck. Given that the coefficient of restitution between the particle and each wall is e show that:

$$(1 + 2e) \tan^2 \theta = e^2$$

4.2 Oblique impact of smooth elastic spheres

When you are studying the collision of two smooth elastic spheres, it is essential to consider separately
(i) the components of the velocities perpendicular to the line of centres at impact
(ii) the components of the velocities parallel to the line of centres at impact.

(i) Since there is no component of the mutual reaction in this direction, then, as before, **the components of the velocities perpendicular to the line of centres are unchanged**.

(ii) It is necessary to form two equations, one expressing **the conservation of momentum in this direction** and the other **Newton's law of restitution for components of velocity in this direction**. This exactly parallels the case of direct impact considered in chapter 5 of Book M2.

Consider two smooth spheres of masses m_1 and m_2, with centres C_1 and C_2, which collide, the coefficient of restitution between the two spheres being e. Just before impact suppose the speed of the first sphere is u_1 at angle α with the line of centres C_1C_2, and the speed of the second sphere is u_2 at angle β with the line of centres C_1C_2.

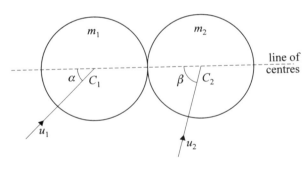

It is helpful to draw a diagram indicating the components of velocities of the spheres *before impact*, along and perpendicular to the line of centres C_1C_2.

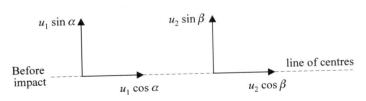

Then draw a diagram indicating the components of velocities of the spheres, *after impact*, along and perpendicular to the line of centres. The components of velocity perpendicular to $C_1 C_2$, namely $u_1 \sin \alpha$ and $u_2 \sin \beta$, are unchanged by the impact. Suppose the components of the velocities along the line of centres after impact are v_1 and v_2 respectively.

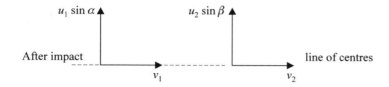

To obtain v_1 and v_2 you need two equations.

(i) Total momentum along $C_1 C_2$ is conserved:

$$m_1 u_1 \cos \alpha + m_2 u_2 \cos \beta = m_1 v_1 + m_2 v_2 \qquad (1)$$

(ii) Newton's law of restitution:

$$\frac{\text{speed of separation along line of centres}}{\text{speed of approach along line of centres}} = e$$

$$\frac{v_2 - v_1}{u_1 \cos \alpha - u_2 \cos \beta} = e$$

or: $$v_2 - v_1 = e(u_1 \cos \alpha - u_2 \cos \beta) \qquad (2)$$

You can solve equations (1) and (2) to find v_1 and v_2. The resultant velocity of each of the spheres and their directions of motion can be found from v_1 and v_2 and the components of velocity perpendicular to $C_1 C_2$, that is, $u_1 \sin \alpha$ and $u_2 \sin \beta$.

Example 5

A smooth sphere A, of mass 2 kg, and moving with speed $8 \, \text{m s}^{-1}$ collides obliquely with a stationary sphere B, of mass 2 kg, the coefficient of restitution between the spheres being $\frac{1}{2}$. At the instant of impact the velocity of A makes an angle of $45°$ with the line of centres of the spheres. Find the magnitude and direction of the velocities of A and B immediately after impact.

The initial situation is summarised in the diagram:

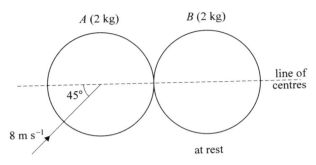

The components of velocity *before impact* are:

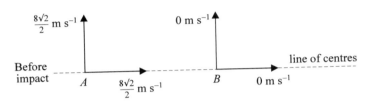

If the speeds of A and B along the line of centres immediately after impact are $v_1 \, \mathrm{m\,s^{-1}}$ and $v_2 \, \mathrm{m\,s^{-1}}$ then the components of velocity *after impact* are:

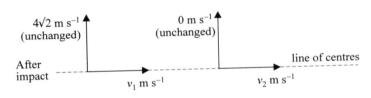

To obtain v_1 and v_2 write down the two usual equations:

(i) Conservation of momentum gives:

$$2(4\sqrt{2} + 0) = 2v_1 + 2v_2$$

or:

$$4\sqrt{2} = v_1 + v_2 \tag{1}$$

(ii) Newton's law of restitution gives:

$$v_2 - v_1 = \tfrac{1}{2}(4\sqrt{2} - 0) \tag{2}$$

Adding (1) and (2) gives:

$$2v_2 = 4\sqrt{2} + 2\sqrt{2} \tag{3}$$

$$v_2 = 3\sqrt{2}$$

Subtracting (2) from (1) gives:

$$2v_1 = 4\sqrt{2} - 2\sqrt{2} \tag{4}$$

$$v_1 = \sqrt{2}$$

For sphere A after impact the components of velocity are:

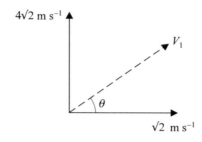

The magnitude of the speed V_1 is obtained from

$$V_1^2 = (4\sqrt{2})^2 + (\sqrt{2})^2 = 32 + 2 = 34$$

so: $\qquad V_1 = \sqrt{34}$

The direction is obtained from:

$$\tan \theta = \frac{4\sqrt{2}}{\sqrt{2}} = 4$$

so: $\qquad\qquad\qquad \theta = 76.0°$

So the speed of A is $\sqrt{34}\,\mathrm{m\,s^{-1}}$, or $5.83\,\mathrm{m\,s^{-1}}$, and the direction makes an angle of $76.0°$ with the line of centres.

For sphere B after impact the components of velocity are:

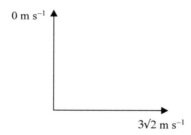

So B moves off along the line of centres with speed $3\sqrt{2}\,\mathrm{m\,s^{-1}}$ or $4.24\,\mathrm{m\,s^{-1}}$.

Example 6

A small smooth sphere A of mass $2\,\mathrm{kg}$ collides with a small smooth sphere B of mass $1\,\mathrm{kg}$. The coefficient of restitution between the spheres is $\frac{1}{2}$. Just before impact A has a speed of $8\,\mathrm{m\,s^{-1}}$ and is moving in a direction inclined at $30°$ to the line of centres and B has a speed of $4\,\mathrm{m\,s^{-1}}$ and is moving in a direction inclined at $60°$ to the line of centres. Find the loss in kinetic energy as a result of the impact. Find also the magnitude of the impulse exerted by B on A.

Here is the situation before impact:

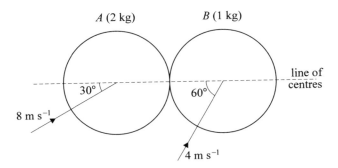

The components of velocity *before impact* are:

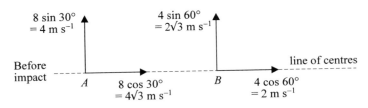

Let the speeds of A and B along the line of centres immediately after impact be $v_1 \,\mathrm{m\,s^{-1}}$ and $v_2 \,\mathrm{m\,s^{-1}}$. The components of velocity after impact are then:

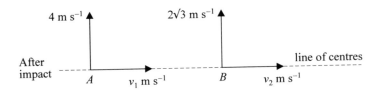

To obtain v_1 and v_2, write down the two usual equations:

(i) Conservation of momentum:

$$2 \times 4\sqrt{3} + 1 \times 2 = 2v_1 + v_2$$

or:
$$8\sqrt{3} + 2 = 2v_1 + v_2 \qquad (1)$$

(ii) Newton's law of restitution:

$$v_2 - v_1 = \tfrac{1}{2}(4\sqrt{3} - 2)$$

or:
$$v_2 - v_1 = 2\sqrt{3} - 1 \qquad (2)$$

Eliminating v_1 between (1) and (2) gives:

$$v_2 = 4\sqrt{3} \qquad (3)$$

Subtracting (2) from (1) gives:

$$3v_1 = 6\sqrt{3} + 3$$
$$v_1 = 2\sqrt{3} + 1 \qquad (4)$$

The velocity components perpendicular to the line of centres are unchanged by the impact. So the loss of kinetic energy is solely due to change in velocities along the line of centres. For sphere A, loss of K.E.

$$= \tfrac{1}{2} \times 2[(4\sqrt{3})^2 - (2\sqrt{3}+1)^2]\,\text{J}$$
$$= [48 - 12 - 1 - 4\sqrt{3}]\,\text{J}$$
$$= (35 - 4\sqrt{3})\,\text{J}$$

For sphere B, loss of K.E.

$$= \tfrac{1}{2} \times 1[(2)^2 - (4\sqrt{3})^2]\,\text{J}$$
$$= \tfrac{1}{2}[4 - 48]\,\text{J}$$
$$= -22\,\text{J}$$

So total loss of K.E. is

$$(13 - 4\sqrt{3})\,\text{J}$$
$$= 6.07\,\text{J}$$

For sphere A, change of momentum along line of centres

$$= 2 \times 4\sqrt{3} - 2(2\sqrt{3}+1)$$
$$= 4\sqrt{3} - 2$$
$$= 4.93\,\text{Ns}$$

Hence the magnitude of the impulse exerted by B on A is 4.93 Ns.

Example 7

A smooth billiard ball A collides with a stationary identical ball B. The direction of motion of A before the impact makes an angle α with the line of centres at the moment of impact. The coefficient of restitution between the two balls is $e(e \neq 1)$. Show that ϕ, the angle through which the direction of motion of A is turned, satisfies

$$\tan \phi = \frac{(1+e)\tan\alpha}{2\tan^2\alpha + 1 - e}$$

Here is the situation just before impact:

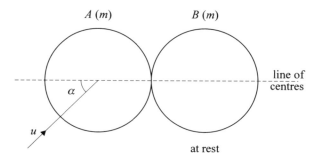

The components of velocity are:

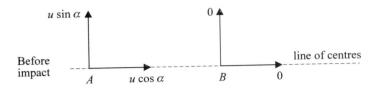

Let the speeds of A and B along the line of centres immediately after impact be v_1 and v_2. The components of velocity are then:

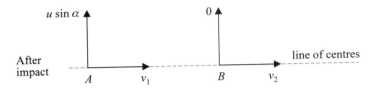

As before, you can get v_1 and v_2 by writing down the usual two equations.

(i) Conservation of momentum:

$$mu \cos \alpha = mv_1 + mv_2$$

or: $$u \cos \alpha = v_1 + v_2 \qquad (1)$$

(ii) Newton's law of restitution:

$$v_2 - v_1 = e(u \cos \alpha - 0)$$

or: $$v_2 - v_1 = eu \cos \alpha \qquad (2)$$

Subtracting (2) from (1) gives:

$$2v_1 = u \cos \alpha - eu \cos \alpha$$

so: $$v_1 = \tfrac{1}{2}u(1 - e) \cos \alpha$$

The components of the velocity of A after impact are:

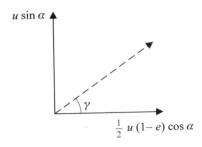

If the new direction of motion of A makes an angle γ with the line of centres, then:

$$\tan \gamma = \frac{u \sin \alpha}{\frac{1}{2} u \cos \alpha (1 - e)}$$

$$= \frac{2 \tan \alpha}{1 - e}$$

As may be seen from the diagram the angle through which the direction of motion of A has turned is

$$(\gamma - \alpha) = \phi$$

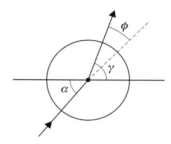

$$\tan \phi = \tan(\gamma - \alpha) = \frac{\tan \gamma - \tan \alpha}{1 + \tan \gamma \tan \alpha}$$

(Book P2 chapter 6)

$$= \frac{\dfrac{2 \tan \alpha}{1 - e} - \tan \alpha}{1 + \dfrac{2 \tan \alpha}{1 - e} \times \tan \alpha}$$

$$= \frac{(1 + e) \tan \alpha}{2 \tan^2 \alpha + 1 - e}$$

Example 8

Two identical smooth spheres are moving on a horizontal table with velocities $(3\mathbf{i} + 4\mathbf{j})\,\mathrm{m\,s^{-1}}$ and $(-\mathbf{i} + \mathbf{j})\,\mathrm{m\,s^{-1}}$. They collide when the line of centres is parallel to the vector $\mathbf{i}$. After impact the velocities are $4\mathbf{j}\,\mathrm{m\,s^{-1}}$ and $(2\mathbf{i} + \mathbf{j})\,\mathrm{m\,s^{-1}}$ respectively. Find the coefficient of restitution between the spheres.

As the information is given here in vector form, you can draw the diagram for velocity components immediately:

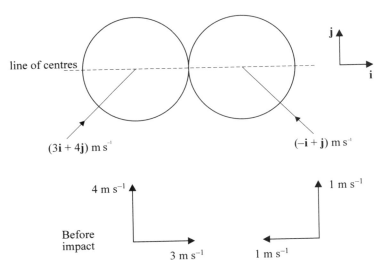

line of centres

$(3\mathbf{i} + 4\mathbf{j})$ m s^{-1} $(-\mathbf{i} + \mathbf{j})$ m s^{-1}

4 m s^{-1} 1 m s^{-1}

Before impact

3 m s^{-1} 1 m s^{-1}

After impact the velocity components are:

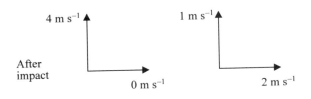

4 m s^{-1} 1 m s^{-1}

After impact

0 m s^{-1} 2 m s^{-1}

Since you want to find e you need only write down the equation that expresses Newton's law of restitution. This gives:

$$(2 - 0) = e[3 - (-1)]$$

So:

$$2 = 4e$$

and:

$$e = \tfrac{1}{2}$$

Exercise 4B

1 A smooth sphere A of mass 2 kg and moving with speed 4 m s^{-1} collides with a stationary sphere B which has the same radius but a mass of 1 kg. The coefficient of restitution between the spheres is $\tfrac{1}{2}$. At the instant of impact the velocity of A makes an angle of 60° with the line of centres. Find the magnitude and

direction of the velocities of A and B and the loss of kinetic energy as a result of the collision.

2 A small smooth sphere A of mass m collides with a stationary sphere B of the same radius but of mass M. At the instant of impact the velocity of A makes an angle of θ with the line of centres. The direction of motion of A is turned through a right angle by the impact. Show that

$$\tan^2 \theta = \frac{eM - m}{M + m}$$

where e is the coefficient of restitution between the spheres.

3

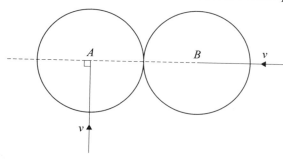

Two identical smooth snooker balls, moving with equal speeds, collide as shown in the diagram. The coefficient of restitution between the balls is $\frac{1}{2}$. Find the speeds and direction of motion of the balls after the collision.

4 Two smooth spheres A and B have equal radii and mass 3 kg and 2 kg respectively. They are moving on a horizontal plane and collide. The coefficient of restitution between the spheres is $\frac{1}{4}$. At the moment of impact the line of centres is parallel to the unit vector $\mathbf{i}$. Immediately before impact the velocity of A is $(8\mathbf{i} + 4\mathbf{j})\,\mathrm{m\,s^{-1}}$ and the velocity of B is $(-4\mathbf{i} + 2\mathbf{j})\,\mathrm{m\,s^{-1}}$.

(a) Find the velocities of A and B immediately after impact.

(b) Find the angle between the velocities of A before and after impact.

(c) Find the loss of kinetic energy as a result of the impact.

5 A smooth billiard ball P, of mass m, moving with speed u, collides with an identical smooth billiard ball Q which is at rest. Just before impact the velocity of P makes an angle θ with the

line of centres. Immediately after impact the velocity of P makes an angle ϕ with the line of centres. Given that the speeds of P and Q immediately after impact are equal, show that $\phi = 2\theta$. Deduce that e, the coefficient of restitution between the balls, is equal to $\tan^2 \theta$.

Find the speeds of P and Q after the impact and the loss of kinetic energy as a result of the impact.

6   A smooth sphere A moving with speed u collides with an identical smooth sphere B at rest. Just before impact the speed of A makes an angle $\alpha(\alpha < \frac{\pi}{2})$ with the line of centres. The coefficient of restitution between the spheres is $\frac{2}{3}$. Find the speeds of A and B after impact and show that if $\sin^2 \alpha = \frac{8}{35}$, the speed of A is halved by the impact.

7   A smooth sphere S of mass m is moving on a horizontal plane when it collides with another smooth sphere T of the same radius but of mass $km(k > 1)$ which is at rest. The sphere S strikes the sphere T obliquely. After the impact the two spheres are moving in perpendicular directions. Show that the coefficient of restitution is equal to $\frac{1}{k}$.

8   Two smooth spheres A and B have equal radii and masses m and $2m$ respectively. Sphere A is moving with velocity $a\mathbf{i} + a\mathbf{j}$ when it strikes sphere B, which is at rest. At the moment of impact the line of centres is parallel to the unit vector $\mathbf{i}$. After the impact the velocities of A and B are $v_1\mathbf{j}$ and $v_2\mathbf{i}$ respectively.
    (a) Show that the coefficient of restitution is $\frac{1}{2}$.
    (b) Find v_1 and v_2 in terms of a.

9   Two small smooth spheres of mass m_1 and m_2, with centres C_1 and C_2, collide obliquely, the coefficient of restitution between the two spheres being e. Just before impact the speed of the first sphere is u_1 at an angle α to C_1C_2 and the speed of the second sphere is u_2 at an angle β to C_1C_2. After the impact the components of the velocities along the line of centres are v_1 and v_2 respectively. Show that

$$v_1 = \frac{(m_1 - em_2)u_1 \cos \alpha + m_2 u_2 (1 + e) \cos \beta}{(m_1 + m_2)}$$

$$v_2 = \frac{m_1 u_1 (1 + e) \cos \alpha + (m_2 - em_1)u_2 \cos \beta}{(m_1 + m_2)}$$

10 Two smooth spheres A and B have equal radii and masses m_1 and m_2 respectively. They are moving on a horizontal plane and collide. Just before impact the speed of A is u_1 and its direction of motion makes an angle α with the line of centres AB. The speed of B is u_2 and its direction of motion makes an angle β with the line of centres AB. Given that the coefficient of restitution between the spheres is e, show that the loss of kinetic energy as a result of the impact is

$$\tfrac{1}{2}\left(\frac{m_1 m_2}{m_1 + m_2}\right)(u_1 \cos \alpha - u_2 \cos \beta)^2 (1 - e^2)$$

SUMMARY OF KEY POINTS

1 **Impact of a smooth sphere on a fixed smooth plane**
   The component of the velocity of the sphere parallel to the plane is unchanged.

   The component of the velocity perpendicular to the plane after impact $= e \times$ the component of the velocity perpendicular to the plane before impact, where e is the coefficient of restitution between the sphere and the plane.

2 **Oblique impact of smooth elastic spheres**
   Perpendicular to line of centres:
   The components of the velocities in this direction are unchanged.

   Parallel to line of centres:
   (i) The linear momentum in this direction is conserved.
   (ii) Speed of separation along line of centres $= e \times$ speed of approach along line of centres (Newton's law of restitution), where e is the coefficient of restitution between the spheres.

Review exercise 2

1   A particle P of mass m moves in a medium which produces a resistance of magnitude mkv, where v is the speed of P and k is a constant. The particle P is projected vertically upwards in this medium with speed $\dfrac{g}{k}$. Show that P comes momentarily to rest after time $\dfrac{\ln 2}{k}$.

Find, in terms of k and g, the greatest height above the point of projection reached by P. [L]

2   A particle of mass m is projected vertically upwards with speed u in a medium which exerts a resisting force of magnitude mkv, where v is the speed of the particle and k is a positive constant. Find the time taken to reach the highest point, and show that the greatest height attained above the point of projection is

$$\frac{1}{k^2}\left[uk - g\ln\left(1 + \frac{ku}{g}\right)\right]$$

Find, in terms of k, g and T, the speed of the particle at time T after it has reached its greatest height, and hence, or otherwise, show that this speed tends to a finite limit as T increases indefinitely. [L]

3   A particle of mass m moves in a straight line on a horizontal table against a resistance of magnitude $\lambda(mv + k)$, where v is the speed and λ and k are positive constants. Given that the particle starts with speed u at time $t = 0$, show that the speed v of the particle at time t is

$$v = \frac{k}{m}(e^{-\lambda t} - 1) + ue^{-\lambda t}$$

[L]

4 A particle, of mass m, moves under gravity down a line of greatest slope of a smooth plane inclined at an angle α to the horizontal. When the speed of the particle is v, the resistance to the motion of the particle is mkv, where k is a positive constant. Show that the limiting speed c of the particle is given by

$$c = \frac{g \sin \alpha}{k}$$

The particle starts from rest. Show that the time T taken to reach a speed of $\frac{1}{2}c$ is given by

$$T = \frac{1}{k} \ln 2$$

Find, in terms of c and k, the distance travelled by the particle in attaining the speed of $\frac{1}{2}c$.

5 A ship, of mass m, is propelled in a straight line through the water by a propeller which develops a constant force of magnitude F. When the speed of the ship is v, the water causes a drag, of magnitude kv, where k is a constant, to act on the ship. The ship starts from rest at time $t = 0$. Show that the ship reaches half its theoretical maximum speed of $\frac{F}{k}$ when

$$t = \frac{(m \ln 2)}{k}.$$

When the ship is moving with speed $\frac{F}{2k}$, an emergency occurs and the captain reverses the engines so that the propeller force, which remains of magnitude F, acts backwards. Show that the ship covers a further distance

$$\frac{mF}{k^2} \left[\frac{1}{2} - \ln\left(\frac{3}{2}\right) \right]$$

on its original course, which may be assumed to remain unchanged, before being brought to rest. [L]

6 A particle is projected vertically upwards with speed U in a medium in which the resistance to motion is proportional to the square of the speed. Given that U is also the speed for which the resistance offered by the medium is equal to the weight of the particle, show that the time of ascent is $\dfrac{\pi U}{4g}$ and that the distance ascended is $\dfrac{U^2}{2g}\ln 2$.   [L]

7 A particle P of mass m moves under gravity in a medium which is such that the resistance to motion is of magnitude mkv^2, where v is the speed of P and k is a positive constant. Show that it is possible for P to fall vertically with a constant speed

$$U = \sqrt{\left(\frac{g}{k}\right)}.$$

Given that P is projected vertically upwards with speed $V(> U)$, show that the speed of P is equal to U when the height of P above the point of projection is

$$\frac{U^2}{2g}\ln\left(\frac{V^2 + U^2}{2U^2}\right)$$

Find, in terms of U, V and g, the time taken for the speed of P to decrease from V to U.   [L]

8 At time t, a particle P, of mass m, moving in a straight line has speed v. The only force acting is a resistance of magnitude $mk(V_0^2 + 2v^2)$, where k is a positive constant and V_0 is the speed of P when $t = 0$. Show that, as v reduces from V_0 to $\dfrac{V_0}{2}$, P travels a distance $\dfrac{\ln 2}{4k}$.

Express the time P takes to cover this distance in the form $\dfrac{\lambda}{kV_0}$, giving the value of λ to two decimal places.   [L]

9 A train, total mass M, including the engine, is moving along a straight horizontal track. The engine exerts a constant driving force of magnitude F. At any instant the total resistance is bv^2 where b is a positive constant and v is the speed of the train at that instant. Show that the limiting speed V of the train is $\left(\dfrac{F}{b}\right)^{\frac{1}{2}}$.

The train starts from rest at $t = 0$. Show that it reaches a speed of $\frac{1}{2}V$ after a time

$$\frac{M}{2bV}\ln 3$$

Show further that the distance covered in this time is

$$\frac{M}{2b}\ln\left(\frac{4}{3}\right) \qquad\qquad [L]$$

10 The equation of motion of a particle moving on the x-axis is

$$\ddot{x} + 2k\dot{x} + n^2 x = 0$$

Given that k and n are positive constants, with $k < n$, show that the time between two successive maxima of $[x]$ is constant.

[L]

11 A particle of mass m is constrained to move along the horizontal straight line Ox. When the particle is at P, where the displacement of P from O is x, the particle is subject to a force of magnitude $m\omega^2|x|$ acting towards O, where ω is a constant. The particle is also subject to a resistance of magnitude $2mk|\dot{x}|$, where k is a positive constant with $k < \omega$.
Show that, at time t,

$$x = \mathrm{e}^{-kt}(A\cos nt + B\sin nt)$$

where A and B are arbitrary constant and $n^2 = \omega^2 - k^2$. Explain why the motion can be regarded as an oscillation about O with period $2\pi/n$ but with decreasing amplitude.
Show that the amplitude decreases by a factor $\mathrm{e}^{-2\pi k/n}$ in one complete oscillation.
In time T, a particle performs an exact number of complete oscillations. The final amplitude is one third of the initial amplitude. Show that

$$kT = \ln 3 \qquad\qquad [L]$$

12 Show that the roots of the equation

$$\lambda^2 + k\lambda + \omega^2 = 0$$

are distinct and both negative when $k > 2\omega > 0$. A particle moves along the x-axis under the action of a force $\omega^2|x|$ per unit mass directed towards the origin and a resisting force kv per unit mass, where k and ω are positive constants and x, v are the displacement from the origin and speed respectively after time t. Show that the differential equation satisifed by x and t is

$$\frac{d^2x}{dt^2} + k\frac{dx}{dt} + \omega^2 x = 0$$

The particle starts from rest when $x = a$. Show that, if $k > 2\omega > 0$,

$$(\lambda_2 - \lambda_1)x = a(\lambda_2 e^{-\lambda_1 t} - \lambda_1 e^{-\lambda_2 t})$$

where $-\lambda_1$, $-\lambda_2$ are the roots of the quadratic equation

$$\lambda^2 + k\lambda + \omega^2 = 0$$

Further, show that the particle does not pass through the origin.

[L]

13 A particle moves on the Ox axis and its displacement x at time t is governed by the equation

$$\frac{d^2x}{dt^2} + 2k\frac{dx}{dt} + n^2 x = 0$$

where k and n are positive constants. Given that $x = a$ and $\frac{dx}{dt} = 0$ when $t = 0$, find x in each of the two cases

(a) $k^2 = 2n^2$

(b) $k^2 = \frac{3}{4}n^2$

Show that in case (b) the time interval between successive stationary values of x is constant. [L]

14 A particle P of mass m is suspended from a fixed point by a spring of natural length l and modulus $2mn^2l$. The particle is projected vertically downards with speed V from its equilibrium position. The motion of the particle is resisted by a force of magnitude $2mn$ times its speed acting in a direction opposite to its motion. Given that x is the displacement of P downwards from the equilibrium position at time t, show that

$$\frac{d^2x}{dt^2} + 2n\frac{dx}{dt} + 2n^2 x = 0$$

Find x in terms of t and sketch the graph of x against t. Show that P is instantaneously at rest when $nt = (k + \frac{1}{4})\pi$, where $k \in \mathbb{N}$. [L]

15 A particle P of mass m is suspend from a fixed point by a light elastic string of natural length a and modulus k^2mg, where k is a positive constant. The particle is released from rest at a distance a below its equilibrium position. The motion of P takes place in a medium which offers a resistance of magnitude

$$kmv\sqrt{\left(\frac{g}{a}\right)}$$

where v is the speed of the particle.
At time t the displacement of P below its equilibrium position is x. Show that, so long as the string remains taut,

$$a\frac{d^2x}{dt^2} + k\sqrt{(ag)}\frac{dx}{dt} + k^2gx = 0$$

Hence show that, while the string remains stretched,

$$x = ae^{-kwt}\left[\cos(kwt\sqrt{3}) + \frac{1}{\sqrt{3}}\sin(kwt\sqrt{3})\right]$$

where $w = \sqrt{\left(\frac{g}{4a}\right)}$.

Deduce that P first comes to rest before the string becomes slack provided that

$$k^2 < e^{\frac{\pi}{\sqrt{3}}}$$

16 A particle of mass m moves in a straight horizontal line and at time t its displacement from a fixed point O on the line is x. The forces acting on the particle are
  (i) a force $-2mk^2x\mathbf{i}$ where $\mathbf{i}$ is a unit vector along Ox,
  (ii) a resistance to the motion of magnitude $3mkv$ where v is the speed of the particle,
  (iii) a force $3mak^2\cos(kt)\mathbf{i}$,
  where a and k are positive constants.
  Write down a differential equation satisifed by x.
  Given that at $t = 0$ the particle is at rest at O, find x at time t.

  [L]

17 A particle P is attached to one end of a spring. The other end of the spring oscillates. The displacement x of P, from a fixed reference point at time t, satisfies the differential equation

$$\frac{d^2x}{dt^2} + 4x = \lambda \sin 4t$$

where λ is a constant. Given that $x = 0$ and $\dfrac{dx}{dt} = \dfrac{\lambda}{3}$ when $t = 0$ obtain x as a function of t.

18 The differential equation for the motion of a particle, which is constrained to move along the x-axis, is

$$\frac{d^2x}{dt^2} + 2k\frac{dx}{dt} + \omega_0^2 x = f(t), \omega_0 > k$$

where ω_0 and k are positive constants. Describe a physical problem for which this could be the differential equation. Obtain the general solution of the equation in the particular case when $f(t) = a\cos\omega t$, where a and ω are positive constants. Find the amplitude of the forced oscillation.

19 A particle P, of mass m kilograms, is fastened to one end of a light spring of natural length L metres and modulus λmg newtons, where λ is a constant. The other end is fixed to the roof of a stationary lift and P is hanging in equilibrium. At time $t = 0$ the lift starts to move vertically upwards with constant speed u metres per second and the distance of P above its initial position after t seconds is y metres.

(a) By considering the total extension in the spring after t seconds show that

$$\frac{d^2y}{dt^2} + k^2 y = k^2 ut$$

where $k^2 = \dfrac{\lambda g}{L}$ and $y = 0, \dfrac{dy}{dt} = 0$ at $t = 0$.

(b) Find y in terms of t and k.
After T seconds, where $T > 0$, a stationary observer outside the lift notices that the particle is instantaneously at rest.

(c) Find the smallest value of T. [L]

20 A particle P, of mass m, is attached to one end of a light elastic string, of natural length L and modulus $8mn^2L$, where n is a constant. The other end of the string is attached to a fixed point O on the horizontal table on which P moves. Initially P is at rest

on the table with $OP = L$. A force is now applied to P in the direction OP. The magnitude of the force is mn^2Le^{-nt} where t is the time measured from the initial application of the force. The motion of P is opposed by a resistance of magnitude $6mn$ times the speed of P. Show that the extension x of the string satisifes the differential equation

$$\frac{d^2x}{dt^2} + 6n\frac{dx}{dt} + 8n^2x = n^2Le^{-nt}$$

Find x in terms of t.

21 A rocket of initial total mass M propels itself by ejecting mass at a constant rate μ per unit time with speed u relative to the rocket. If the rocket is at rest directed vertically upwards, show that it will not initially leave the ground unless $\mu u > Mg$. Assuming this condition to hold, show that the velocity of the rocket after time t is given by

$$-u\ln\left(1 - \frac{\mu t}{M}\right) - gt$$

Show also that when the mass of the rocket has been reduced to half the initial value its height above the ground will be

$$\frac{uM}{2\mu}\left(1 - \ln 2 - \frac{Mg}{4\mu u}\right)$$

22 A raindrop falls through a stationary cloud. Its mass m increases by accretion uniformly with the distance x fallen, so that

$$m = m_0(1 + kx)$$

Given that its speed v is zero when $x = 0$, show that

$$v^2 = \frac{2g}{3k}\left[1 + kx - \frac{1}{(1 + kx)^2}\right]$$

23 A particle whose initial mass is m is projected vertically upwards at time $t = 0$ with speed gT, where T is a constant. At time t its speed is u and its mass has increased to $me^{\frac{t}{T}}$. If the added mass is at rest when it is acquired, show that

$$\frac{\mathrm{d}}{\mathrm{d}t}(mu\mathrm{e}^{1/T}) = -mg\mathrm{e}^{1/T}$$

Deduce that the mass of the particle at its highest point is $2m$. If, instead, the added mass is falling with constant speed gT when it is acquired find the mass of the particle at its highest point.

[L]

24 A raindrop is observed at time $t = 0$ when it has mass m and downward velocity u. As it falls under gravity its mass increases by condensation at a constant rate λ and a resisting force acts on it, proportional to its speed and equal to λv when the speed is v. Show that

$$\frac{\mathrm{d}}{\mathrm{d}t}(M^2 v) = M^2 g$$

where $M = m + \lambda t$, and find the speed of the raindrop at time t.

25 A particle falls from rest under gravity through a stationary cloud. The mass of the particle increases by accretion from the cloud at a rate which at any time is mkv, where m is the mass and v the speed of the particle and k is a constant. Show that after the particle has fallen a distance x

$$kv^2 = g(1 - \mathrm{e}^{-2kx})$$

and find the distance the particle has fallen after time t.

26 Two equal smooth spheres approach each other from opposite directions with equal speeds. The coefficient of restitution between the spheres is e. At the moment of impact, their common normal is inclined at an angle θ to the original direction of motion. Given that after impact each sphere moves at right angles to its original direction of motion, prove that

$$\tan\theta = \sqrt{e}$$

[L]

27 A smooth uniform sphere A, of mass $2m$, is at rest on a smooth horizontal table. A second smooth sphere B, of mass m and the same radius, is moving with speed u and collides with the first sphere. At impact the direction of motion of sphere B makes an angle of $45°$ with the line of centres of the two spheres. The coefficient of restitution is $\frac{1}{2}$. Show that after impact the

direction of motion of sphere B is perpendicular to the line of centres. Show also that the loss of kinetic energy due to the collision is $\frac{1}{8}mu^2$. [L]

28 A smooth sphere A, of mass m and radius a, moves on a horizontal table with speed u and collides with a smooth stationary sphere B, of mass $\lambda m (\lambda > 1)$ and radius a. Before impact the direction of motion of A makes an acute angle θ with the line of centres of the spheres. As a result of the impact A is deflected through a right angle. The coefficient of restitution between the spheres is e.

Prove that $e > \dfrac{1}{\lambda}$ and show that

$$\tan^2\theta \leqslant \frac{\lambda - 1}{\lambda + 1}$$

Given that $\lambda = 5$ and $\theta = \dfrac{\pi}{6}$, find e and the kinetic energy lost as a result of the impact. [L]

29 Two smooth billiard balls A and B each of radius a have mass m and M respectively. B is initially at rest and A approaches it with speed u. The perpendicular distance of the centre of B from the line of motion of the centre of A is d. The coefficient of restitution between the spheres is e. Show that the kinetic energy lost due to the impact is

$$\frac{mMu^2}{2(m+M)}(1 - e^2)\left(1 - \frac{d^2}{4a^2}\right)$$ [L]

30 A smooth circular horizontal table is surrounded by a smooth rim whose interior surface is vertical. AB is a diameter of the circle.

Two equal particles of mass m are projected simultaneously from A each with speed V in directions making angles of $30°$ with AB, one on each side of the diameter. After only one impact each at the rim, the particles meet at a point P on AB where $AP < AB$.

(a) Show that the coefficient of restitution e between each particle and the rim satisfies $e > \frac{1}{3}$.

When the particles meet, they coalesce.

(b) Find the speed of the combined particle, in terms of e and V.

(c) Given that the kinetic energy of the combined particle is $\frac{1}{16}mV^2$, find the value of e. [L]

31 A smooth sphere A collides with an identical stationary sphere B so that the angle between the velocity of A and the line of centres of the spheres is α immediately before the collision and β immediately afterwards. Show that

$$2\tan\alpha = (1-e)\tan\beta$$

where e is the coefficient of restitution.

Show also that, as α varies but e remains fixed, the maximum deflection that can be produced in the direction of motion of A is δ, where

$$\sqrt{(8-8e)}\tan\delta = (1+e)$$

[L]

32 Two smooth spheres A and B of equal radius, but of mass $3m$ and $2m$ respectively, moving on a smooth horizontal table collide. At the moment of impact the line joining their centres is parallel to the unit vector $\mathbf{i}$. The unit vector $\mathbf{j}$ is in the plane of the table and is perpendicular to $\mathbf{i}$. Immediately before collision the velocities of A and B are $u(4\mathbf{i}+2\mathbf{j})$ and $u(-2\mathbf{i}+\mathbf{j})$ respectively, where u is a positive constant. Given that the coefficient of restitution between the spheres is $\frac{1}{4}$, find

(a) the velocities of A and B immediately after impact

(b) the cosine of the angle between the velocities of A before and after impact

(c) the kinetic energy lost as a result of the impact.

After impact, sphere B receives an impulsive blow which brings it to rest. Find the impulse of the blow. [L]

33 A smooth sphere A rests on a smooth horizontal floor at a distance d from a plane vertical wall. An identical sphere B is projected along the floor with speed V towards the wall in a direction perpendicular to the wall. Before striking the wall, sphere B strikes sphere A so that the line of centres on impact is inclined at an angle α to the wall. The coefficient of restitution between the spheres is $\frac{2}{3}$. Show that the components of the velocity of B after impact, along and perpendicular to the line of centres, are $\dfrac{V \sin \alpha}{6}$ and $V \cos \alpha$.

Given that the diameter of either sphere is negligible compared to d, show also that the distance between the points where the spheres strike the wall is

$$\frac{6d \cot \alpha}{1 + 5 \cos^2 \alpha}$$

[L]

Examination style paper

M3

Answer all questions   **Time 90 minutes**

Whenever a numerical value of g is required, take $g = 9.8 \, \text{m s}^{-2}$.

1 A particle P of mass m falls from rest in a medium that produces a resistance of magnitude mkv, where k is a constant, when the speed of the particle is v. Show that when P has reached a speed of V it will have fallen for a time

$$\frac{1}{k} \ln \left(\frac{g}{g - kV} \right)$$

(7 marks)

2 A pulley in the form of a uniform disc of mass $4m$ has centre O and radius a. It is free to rotate in a vertical plane about a fixed smooth horizontal axis through O. A light inextensible string has one end attached to a point on the rim of the pulley and is wrapped several times round the rim. The length of the string not wrapped round the rim is $8a$ and has a particle P, of mass m, attached at its free end. Initially the disc is at rest and P is held close to the rim of the disc and level with O. The particle P is now released. Determine the angular speed of the disc immediately after the string becomes taut.

(8 marks)

3 A rocket has initial total mass M. It propels itself by ejecting mass at a constant rate k per unit time with speed u relative to the rocket. The rocket is initially at rest directed vertically upwards. Obtain the differential equation satisfied by the speed v at time t and hence show that the rocket will not leave the launch pad unless $ku > Mg$.

(9 marks)

4 Prove, using integration, that the moment of inertia of a uniform solid sphere, of mass M and radius r, about a diameter is $\frac{2}{5}Mr^2$. Hence obtain the moment of inertia of a uniform solid hemisphere, of mass m and radius r, about a diameter of its plane face.

(10 marks)

5 A ring of mass m and radius a has a particle of mass m attached to it at the point A. The ring can rotate about a fixed smooth horizontal axis which is tangential to the ring at the point B which is diametrically opposite A. The system is released from rest with AB horizontal. Find the angular speed of the system when AB has turned through an angle $\frac{\pi}{6}$.

(10 marks)

6 A car has mass 800 kg and is driven by an engine which generates a constant power of 10 kW. The only resistance to the car's motion is air resistance, which is of magnitude $8v^2$ N when the speed of the car is v m s^{-1}. Find the distance travelled as the car's speed increases from 2 m s^{-1} to 10 m s^{-1}.

(11 marks)

7

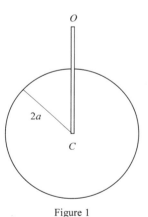

Figure 1

Figure 1 shows a compound pendulum consisting of a thin uniform rod OC, of length $3a$ and mass M, rigidly attached at C to the centre of a uniform disc of radius $2a$ and mass M. The rod OC is in the same vertical plane as the disc. The pendulum is free to rotate in this vertical plane about a fixed smooth horizontal axis through O perpendicular to the plane of the disc.

(a) Show that the moment of inertia of the pendulum about the axis through O is $14Ma^2$.

Given that the pendulum performs small oscillations about its position of stable equilibrium,

(b) find, in terms of g and a, the period of oscillation.

(11 marks)

8

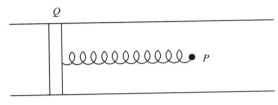

Figure 2

Figure 2 shows a particle P of mass 1 kg which is free to slide horizontally inside a smooth cylindrical tube. The particle is attached to one end of a light elastic spring of natural length 0.5 m and modulus of elasticity 2 N. The system is initially at rest. The other end Q of the spring is then forced to oscillate with simple harmonic motion so that at time t seconds its displacement from its initial position is $\frac{1}{4}\sin 3t$ metres. The displacement of P from its initial position at time t seconds is x metres, measured in the same direction as the displacement of Q.

(a) Show that $\dfrac{d^2x}{dt^2} + 4x = \sin 3t$.

(b) Find the first time, after the motion starts, at which P is instantaneously at rest.

(16 marks)

9 A uniform small smooth sphere A, of mass m, moving with speed u on a smooth horizontal table collides with a stationary uniform small smooth sphere B of the same size as A and of mass m. The direction of motion of A before the impact makes an angle α with the line of centres of A and B, and the direction of motion of A after impact makes an angle β with the same line as shown in Fig. 3.

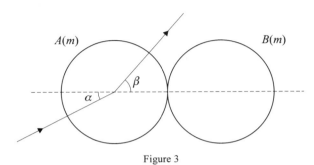

Figure 3

Given that the coefficient of restitution between the spheres is $\frac{1}{3}$:

(a) Show that $\tan \beta = 3 \tan \alpha$.

(b) Express $\tan(\beta - \alpha)$ in terms of t where $t = \tan \alpha$.

(c) Hence find, as α varies, the maximum angle of deflection of A caused by the impact.

(18 marks)

Answers

The University of London Examination and Assessment Council accepts no responsibility whatsoever for the accuracy or method of working in the answers given for examination questions.

Exercise 1A

1 $\dfrac{4ma^2}{3}$, $\dfrac{2a\sqrt{3}}{3}$

2 $\dfrac{m}{3}(l^2 - 3la + 3a^2)$, $\sqrt{\left(\dfrac{l^2 - 3la + 3a^2}{3}\right)}$

3 $\frac{1}{3}ml^2 \sin^2\theta$, $\dfrac{\sqrt{3}}{3}l\sin\theta$

4 $\frac{1}{6}mb^2$, $\frac{1}{6}b\sqrt{6}$

5 $\frac{16}{5}ma^2$, $\dfrac{4a\sqrt{5}}{5}$ 6 $7mr^2$

7 $\frac{1}{3}ml^2$ 8 $\frac{1}{12}ml^2$

9 $\frac{11}{9}ma^2$ 10 $\frac{41}{72}md^2$ 11 $\frac{5}{2}ml^2$

12 $\dfrac{Mr^2(2h + r)}{2(h + r)}$,   13 $\frac{1}{3}m(a^2 + b^2)$

14 $\frac{1}{2}Mr^2$

Exercise 1B

1 $\frac{3}{10}mr^2$ 2 $\frac{3}{2}mr^2$ 3 $\frac{1}{4}mr^2$, $\frac{5}{4}mr^2$

4 md^2

5 (a) $\frac{16}{3}ma^2$ (b) $\frac{40}{3}ma^2$ (c) $\frac{28}{3}ma^2$

6 (a) $\frac{29}{3}mr^2$ (b) $\frac{41}{3}mr^2$ (c) $\frac{79}{6}mr^2$

(d) $\frac{173}{18}mr^2$

7 $\frac{1}{12}m(a^2 + 4b^2)$ 8 $r\sqrt{(\frac{3}{2})}$

10 $\dfrac{8\sqrt{3}}{3}$ 11 $\dfrac{7mr^2}{5}$ 12 $\frac{1}{4}\sqrt{6}$

13 (a) $\frac{5}{2}ma^2$ (b) $\frac{13}{2}ma^2$

14 $\frac{1}{3}ma^2$

Exercise 2A

1 8 J   2 1.58 J, 1.58 J

3 (a) 4.35 J   (b) 4.08 J

4 (a) 14.7 J   (b) 4.43 rad s^{-1}

(c) 6.26 rad s^{-1}

5 2.56 rad s^{-1} particle

6 (a) $\sqrt{\left(\dfrac{6g}{13l}\right)}$ (b) 1.65^c 7 0.506^c

8 (a) $4\sqrt{\left(\dfrac{3g}{19l}\right)}$ (b) $12\sqrt{\left(\dfrac{g}{19l}\right)}$ (c) $\dfrac{\pi}{3}$

9 (a) $\dfrac{9l}{8}$ (b) $\frac{243}{128}mgl$

10 $\sqrt{\left(\dfrac{g}{a}\right)}$ rad s^{-1} 11 $\sqrt{\left(\dfrac{2mgh}{M + m}\right)}$

12 $k > 3$, uniform lamina

Exercise 2B

1 $\dfrac{15g}{2a}$ 2 0.25 N   3 5 N, 1.04 kg

4 (a) $\dfrac{2g}{5a}$ (b) $\dfrac{2g}{5a}\cos\theta$

5 3.06 N   3.68 N   4.9 rad s^{-2}

6 (a) $\dfrac{13mg}{7}$ (b) $\dfrac{\sqrt{217}}{14}mg$

7 (a) $\sqrt{\left(\dfrac{3g(1 - \cos\theta)}{7a}\right)}$ (b) $\dfrac{19mg}{7}$

8 (a) $mg\left(4\sqrt{2} - \dfrac{3}{2}\right), \dfrac{mg}{4}$

   (b) $0, mg(\sqrt{2} - 1)$

9 (a) $\dfrac{2mg}{5}, -\dfrac{14mg}{15}$ (b) $0, \dfrac{19mg}{5}$

Exercise 2C

1 $15\,\text{N m s}$ **2** $\frac{1}{2}\text{N m s}$

3 $\dfrac{7}{34}\sqrt{\left(\dfrac{6g}{7a}\right)}\,\text{rad s}^{-1}$ 0.322^{c}

4 $5.42\,\text{rad s}^{-1},\ 7.23\,\text{N s}$

5 $2m\sqrt{\left(\dfrac{ga}{3}\right)}, \dfrac{\pi}{3}$ **6** $0.537\,\text{m}$

7 $2.86\,\text{rad s}^{-1}$ **8** $a(4 - \sqrt{2})$

9 $\dfrac{27u}{8a}$ **10** $\dfrac{18v}{13l}$ **11** $68.1m\sqrt{(gl)}$, yes.

Exercise 2D

1 $4\pi\sqrt{\left(\dfrac{a}{3g}\right)}, \dfrac{4a}{3}$ **2** $4\pi\sqrt{\left(\dfrac{10a}{21g}\right)}, \dfrac{40a}{21}$

3 $2\pi\sqrt{\left(\dfrac{d}{g}\right)}, d$ **4** $2\pi\sqrt{\left(\dfrac{a\sqrt{3}}{g}\right)}, a\sqrt{3}$

5 $3.28\,\text{s}, 2\frac{2}{3}\text{m}$ **6** $2\pi\sqrt{\left(\dfrac{3r}{2g}\right)}, \dfrac{3r}{2}$

7 $4\pi\sqrt{\left(\dfrac{a}{3g}\right)}\quad \dfrac{11m}{3}$

8 (a) $2\pi\sqrt{\left(\dfrac{Ma^2 + 3mx^2}{3mgx}\right)}$ (c) $a\sqrt{\left(\dfrac{M}{3m}\right)}$

9 (b) $6a$ **10** $\frac{146}{15}ma^2, 2.99a$

Review Exercise 1

1 $\frac{1}{4}ma^2, \frac{5}{4}ma^2$ **2** $\frac{2}{3}Ma^2$

3 (a) $\frac{7}{2}Ma^2$ (b) $\frac{9}{4}Ma^2$

4 (a) $\sqrt{\dfrac{13}{8}}$ (b) $\dfrac{7\sqrt{2}}{8}$

6 $\dfrac{2V^2}{3g}, \dfrac{3g}{4}, \dfrac{3mg}{4}$ **7** $109\,\text{rpm}$

8 $2.03\,\text{kg m}^2$ **9** $\left(\dfrac{2\sqrt{3}g}{3l}\right)^{\frac{1}{2}}$

10 $\left(\dfrac{2mgx}{M + m}\right)^{\frac{1}{2}}$

11 $\left(\dfrac{6g(\sqrt{2} - 1)}{5a}\right)^{\frac{1}{2}}, (2.2 - 0.6\sqrt{2})Mg$

12 $\frac{8}{3}ma^2, \frac{5}{2}mg\cos\theta + m\sqrt{2a\omega^2} - \frac{3}{2}mg$
   $\frac{1}{4}mg\sin\theta$

13 $\frac{5}{2}Mg\sin\theta, \frac{1}{4}Mg\cos\theta$

14 $\frac{4}{7}mg\cos\theta, \frac{13}{7}mg\sin\theta$ **16** $\dfrac{3v}{4a}$

17 $\dfrac{Ma^2}{2}, \left(\dfrac{8g}{5a}\right)^{\frac{1}{2}}, \dfrac{4u}{9a} + \dfrac{5}{9}\left(\dfrac{8g}{5a}\right)^{\frac{1}{2}}$

18 $\dfrac{3Vd}{3d^2 + 8a^2}$ **19** $\sqrt{\left(\dfrac{4g}{7a}\right)}$

20 (a) $\dfrac{3Ma^2}{2}$ (b) $\dfrac{Ma^2}{4}$ (c) $\pi\sqrt{\left(\dfrac{6a}{g}\right)}$

   (d) $\pi\sqrt{\left(\dfrac{5a}{g}\right)}$

21 $\dfrac{4\pi^2(12a^2 - 14ax + 5x^2)}{(7a - 5x)g}$

22 $\dfrac{7ma^2}{5}, \sqrt{\left(\dfrac{10ga}{7}\right)}$

23 $\frac{3}{2}ma^2, 2\sqrt{\left(\dfrac{ga}{3}\right)}, 2\pi\sqrt{\left(\dfrac{3a}{2g}\right)}$

24 $\left(\dfrac{2(4a^2 - 5ax + 2x^2)}{g(5a - 4x)}\right)^{\frac{1}{2}}$

25 (a) $\dfrac{5a}{6}$ (b) $\sqrt{\left(\dfrac{2g}{3a}\right)}$

   (c) $2\pi\sqrt{\left(\dfrac{6a}{5g}\right)}$

26 $2\pi\sqrt{\left(\dfrac{5a}{6g}\right)}$

27 (a) No   (b) Yes; $\pi\sqrt{\left(\dfrac{3\pi a}{2\sqrt{2}g}\right)}$

28 $\sqrt{7} : \sqrt{2}$

Exercise 3A

1. $t = \ln 7 = 1.95$

2. (a) $x = \frac{4}{3} - \frac{4}{9}\ln 4 = 0.717$
   (b) $v = 14\,e^{-1.5} - 2 = 1.12$

3. (a) $\frac{1}{2}\ln(51)$ metres $= 1.97\,\text{m}$
   (b) $(102e^{-2} - 2)^{\frac{1}{2}}\,\text{m s}^{-1} = 3.44\,\text{m s}^{-1}$

4. (a) $\frac{1}{3}\arctan(2)$ seconds $= 0.369\,\text{s}$
   (b) $\frac{1}{3}\ln 5$ metres $= 0.536\,\text{m}$

6. $\dfrac{1}{19.6k}\ln\left(1 + \dfrac{ku^2}{\mu}\right)\,\text{m}$;

   $\dfrac{1}{9.8\sqrt{(k\mu)}}\arctan\left[u\sqrt{\left(\dfrac{k}{\mu}\right)}\right]\,\text{s}$

7. (a) $\left[\dfrac{g}{k}(1 - e^{-2kd}) + u^2 e^{-2kd}\right]^{\frac{1}{2}}$
   (b) $(u^2 + 2gd)^{\frac{1}{2}}$

10. $6.38\,\text{m}$

11. $\dfrac{m}{3k}\ln\left(\dfrac{63}{37}\right)$

Exercise 3B

1. $x = e^{-\frac{\pi}{2}}$; damped oscillatory motion

2. $x = 4e^{-t}(1 + t)$; $8e^{-2}\,\text{m s}^{-1}$

3. $x = e^{-t}(2\cos 2t + \sin 2t)$

4. $x = 2e^{-t} - e^{-2t}$, $t = \ln(10 + 3\sqrt{10})$

6. (a) $x = \dfrac{u}{3k}\,e^{-kt}\sin 3kt$

9. $x = \dfrac{\lambda}{6}\sin 2t + \dfrac{\lambda}{3}\sin t$

10. $x = \dfrac{V}{6n}(8 - 9e^{-nt} + e^{-3nt})$

11. (a) $\ddot{x} + k\dot{x} + \omega^2 x = ku$

Execise 3C

1. If given condition is not satisfied the rocket will not lift off the ground.

2. $x = \dfrac{g}{4k}\left[at + \frac{1}{2}kt^2 + \dfrac{a^4}{2k(a + kt)^2} - \dfrac{a^2}{2k}\right]$

Exercise 4A

1. $17.8\,\text{m s}^{-1}$, $13°$ to wall

2. $6.32\,\text{m s}^{-1}$, $14.1°$ to wall

3. (a) $(3\mathbf{i} + 2\mathbf{j})\,\text{m s}^{-1}$ (b) $27\,\text{J}$
   (c) $18\mathbf{i}\,\text{N s}$

4. (a) $(2\mathbf{i} + 3\mathbf{j})\,\text{m s}^{-1}$ (b) $18\mathbf{j}\,\text{N s}$

Exercise 4B

1. speed of $A = \sqrt{13}\,\text{m s}^{-1}$, $\arctan(2\sqrt{3})$ to line of centres
   speed of $B = 2\,\text{m s}^{-1}$ along line of centres
   loss of K.E. $= 1\,\text{J}$

3. sphere centre A : speed $\dfrac{5V}{4}$, making angle $127°$ with AB
   sphere centre B : speed $\dfrac{V}{4}$, along AB

4. (a) $v_A = (2\mathbf{i} + 4\mathbf{j})\,\text{m s}^{-1}$,
   $v_B = (5\mathbf{i} + 2\mathbf{j})\,\text{m s}^{-1}$
   (b) $36.9°$ (c) $81\,\text{J}$

5. speed $= \dfrac{u}{2}(1 + e)^{\frac{1}{2}}$,
   loss of K.E. $= \frac{1}{4}mu^2(1 - e)$

6. speed of $A = \frac{1}{2}u(4\sin^2\alpha + \frac{1}{9}\cos^2\alpha)^{\frac{1}{2}}$
   speed of $B = \frac{5}{6}u\cos\alpha$

8. (b) $v_1 = a$, $v_2 = \dfrac{a}{2}$

Review Exercise 2

1. $\dfrac{g}{k^2}(1 - \ln 2)$

2. $\dfrac{1}{k}\ln\left(1 + \dfrac{ku}{g}\right)$; $\dfrac{g}{k}(1 - e^{-kT})$

4. $\dfrac{c}{k}\left(\ln 2 - \frac{1}{2}\right)$

7. $\dfrac{U}{g}\left[\arctan\left(\dfrac{V}{U}\right) - \dfrac{\pi}{4}\right]$

8. $\lambda = 0.24$

13. (a) $x = \frac{1}{2}a(1 + \sqrt{2})e^{(1-\sqrt{2})nt} + \frac{1}{2}a(1 - \sqrt{2})\,e^{-(1+\sqrt{2})nt}$
    (b) $x = 2ae^{-nt\frac{\sqrt{3}}{2}}(\cos\frac{1}{2}nt + \sqrt{3}\sin\frac{1}{2}nt)$

14. $\dfrac{V}{n}e^{-nt}\cos\left(nt + \dfrac{\pi}{2}\right)$

16 $\ddot{x} + 3k\dot{x} + 2k^2x = 3ak^2\cos(kt)$

$x = \dfrac{6a}{5}e^{-2kt} - \dfrac{3a}{2}e^{-kt} + \dfrac{3a}{10}\cos kt$
$\quad + \dfrac{9a}{10}\sin kt$

17 $x = \dfrac{\lambda}{3}\sin 2t - \dfrac{\lambda}{12}\sin 4t$

18 $\dfrac{a}{[(\omega^2 - \omega_0^2)^2 + 4k^2\omega^2]^{\frac{1}{2}}}$

19 (b) $y = u\left(t - \dfrac{1}{k}\sin kt\right)$ (c) $T = \dfrac{2\pi}{k}$

20 $x = L(-\tfrac{1}{2}e^{-2nt} + \tfrac{1}{6}e^{-4nt} + \tfrac{1}{3}e^{-nt})$

23 $\tfrac{3}{2}m$

24 $\dfrac{g}{3\lambda}\left[m + \lambda t - \dfrac{m^3}{(m + \lambda t)^2}\right] + \dfrac{m^2 u}{(m + \lambda t)^2}$

25 $\dfrac{1}{k}\ln\cosh\left[t\sqrt{\left(\dfrac{g}{k}\right)}\right]$

28 $e = \tfrac{3}{5}$, K.E. lost $= \tfrac{1}{5}mu^2$

30 (b) $\dfrac{V\sqrt{3}}{4}(1 - e)$ (c) $\dfrac{3 - \sqrt{3}}{3} = 0.42$

32 (a) $u(\mathbf{i} + 2\mathbf{j})$, $u(2\tfrac{1}{2}\mathbf{i} + \mathbf{j})$

  (b) $\tfrac{4}{5}$

  (c) $20\tfrac{1}{4}mu^2$

  $-mu(5\mathbf{i} + 2\mathbf{j})$

Examination style paper

2 $\dfrac{4}{3}\sqrt{\left(\dfrac{g}{a}\right)}$

3 $\dfrac{dv}{dt} = \dfrac{ku - (M - kt)g}{M - kt}$

4 $\tfrac{2}{5}mr^2$ **5** $\sqrt{\left(\dfrac{6g}{11a}\right)}$ **6** 53.4 m

7 $\dfrac{4\pi}{3}\sqrt{\left(\dfrac{7a}{g}\right)}$ **8** $\dfrac{2\pi}{5}$

9 $\dfrac{2t}{1 + 3t^2}$, maximum deflection $30°$

List of symbols and notation

The following symbols and notation are used in the London modular mathematics examinations:

$\{ \quad \}$	the set of
$\mathrm{n}(A)$	the number of elements in the set A
$\{x: \quad \}$	the set of all x such that
$\in$	is an element of
$\notin$	is not an element of
$\varnothing$	the empty (null) set
$\mathscr{E}$	the universal set
$\cup$	union
$\cap$	intersection
$\subset$	is a subset of
A'	the complement of the set A
PQ	operation Q followed by operation P
$\mathrm{f}: A \rightarrow B$	f is a function under which each element of set A has an image in set B
$\mathrm{f}: x \mapsto y$	f is a function under which x is mapped to y
$\mathrm{f}(x)$	the image of x under the function f
f^{-1}	the inverse relation of the function f
fg	the function f of the function g
○——○	open interval on the number line
●——●	closed interval on the number line
$\mathbb{N}$	the set of positive integers and zero, $\{0, 1, 2, 3, \ldots\}$
$\mathbb{Z}$	the set of integers, $\{0, \pm 1, \pm 2, \pm 3, \ldots\}$
$\mathbb{Z}^+$	the set of positive integers, $\{1, 2, 3, \ldots\}$
$\mathbb{Q}$	the set of rational numbers
$\mathbb{Q}^+$	the set of positive rational numbers, $\{x: x \in \mathbb{Q}, x > 0\}$
$\mathbb{R}$	the set of real numbers
$\mathbb{R}^+$	the set of positive real numbers, $\{x: x \in \mathbb{R}, x > 0\}$
$\mathbb{R}_0^+$	the set of positive real numbers and zero, $\{x: x \in \mathbb{R}, x \geqslant 0\}$
$\mathbb{C}$	the set of complex numbers
$\sqrt{\ }$	the positive square root
$[a, b]$	the interval $\{x: a \leqslant x \leqslant b\}$
$(a, b]$	the interval $\{x: a < x \leqslant b\}$
(a, b)	the interval $\{x: a < x < b\}$

$\lvert x \rvert$	the modulus of $x = \begin{cases} x \text{ for } x \geqslant 0 \\ -x \text{ for } x < 0 \end{cases}, x \in \mathbb{R}$
$\approx$	is approximately equal to
$\mathbf{A}^{-1}$	the inverse of the non-singular matrix A
$\mathbf{A}^{\mathrm{T}}$	the transpose of the matrix A
$\det \mathbf{A}$	the determinant of the square matrix A
$\displaystyle\sum_{r=1}^{n} \mathrm{f}(r)$	$\mathrm{f}(1) + \mathrm{f}(2) + \ldots + \mathrm{f}(n)$
$\displaystyle\prod_{r=1}^{n} \mathrm{f}(r)$	$\mathrm{f}(1)\mathrm{f}(2)\ldots\mathrm{f}(n)$
$\displaystyle\binom{n}{r}$	the binomial coefficient $\dfrac{n!}{r!(n-r)!}$ for $n \in \mathbb{Z}^{+}$ $\quad\dfrac{n(n-1)\ldots(n-r+1)}{r!}$ for $n \in \mathbb{Q}$
$\exp x$	e^{x}
$\ln x$	the natural logarithm of $x, \log_{\mathrm{e}} x$
$\lg x$	the common logarithm of $x, \log_{10} x$
$\arcsin$	the inverse function of sin with range $[-\pi/2, \pi/2]$
$\arccos$	the inverse function of cos with range $[0, \pi]$
$\arctan$	the inverse function of tan with range $(-\pi/2, \pi/2)$
arsinh	the inverse function of sinh with range $\mathbb{R}$
arcosh	the inverse function of cosh with range $\mathbb{R}_{0}^{+}$
artanh	the inverse function of tanh with range $\mathbb{R}$
$\mathrm{f}'(x), \mathrm{f}''(x), \mathrm{f}'''(x)$	the first, second and third derivatives of $\mathrm{f}(x)$ with respect to x
$\mathrm{f}^{(r)}(x)$	the rth derivative of $\mathrm{f}(x)$ with respect to x
$\dot{x}, \ddot{x}, \ldots$	the first, second, . . . derivatives of x with respect to t
z	a complex number, $z = x + \mathrm{i}y = r(\cos\theta + \mathrm{i}\sin\theta) = r\mathrm{e}^{\mathrm{i}\theta}$
$\operatorname{Re} z$	the real part of z, $\operatorname{Re} z = x = r\cos\theta$
$\operatorname{Im} z$	the imaginary part of z, $\operatorname{Im} z = y = r\sin\theta$
z^{*}	the conjugate of $z, z^{*} = x - \mathrm{i}y = r(\cos\theta - \mathrm{i}\sin\theta) = r\mathrm{e}^{-\mathrm{i}\theta}$
$\lvert z \rvert$	the modulus of $z, \lvert z \rvert = \sqrt{(x^{2} + y^{2})} = r$
$\arg z$	the principal value of the argument of z, $\arg z = \theta$, where $\left.\begin{array}{l}\sin\theta = y/r \\ \cos\theta = x/r\end{array}\right\} -\pi < \theta \leqslant \pi$
$\mathbf{a}$	the vector $\mathbf{a}$
$\overrightarrow{AB}$	the vector represented in magnitude and direction by the directed line segment AB
$\hat{\mathbf{a}}$	a unit vector in the direction of $\mathbf{a}$
$\mathbf{i}, \mathbf{j}, \mathbf{k}$	unit vectors in the directions of the cartesian coordinate axes
$\lvert \mathbf{a} \rvert$	the magnitude of $\mathbf{a}$
$\lvert \overrightarrow{AB} \rvert$	the magnitude of $\overrightarrow{AB}$
$\mathbf{a}.\mathbf{b}$	the scalar product of $\mathbf{a}$ and $\mathbf{b}$
$\mathbf{a} \times \mathbf{b}$	the vector product of $\mathbf{a}$ and $\mathbf{b}$

A'	the complement of the event A
$\mathrm{P}(A)$	probability of the event A
$\mathrm{P}(A|B)$	probability of the event A conditional on the event B
$\mathrm{E}(X)$	the mean (expectation, expected value) of the random variable X
$X, Y, R,$ etc.	random variables
$x, y, r,$ etc.	values of the random variables $X, Y, R,$ etc.
$x_1, x_2 \ldots$	observations
$f_1, f_2, \ldots$	frequencies with which the observations $x_1, x_2, \ldots$ occur
$\mathrm{p}(x)$	probability function $\mathrm{P}(X = x)$ of the discrete random variable X
$p_1, p_2, \ldots$	probabilities of the values $x_1, x_2, \ldots$ of the discrete random variable X
$\mathrm{f}(x), \mathrm{g}(x), \ldots$	the value of the probability density function of a continuous random variable X
$\mathrm{F}(x), \mathrm{G}(x), \ldots$	the value of the (cumulative) distribution function $\mathrm{P}(X \leqslant x)$ of a continuous random variable X
$\mathrm{Var}(X)$	variance of the random variable X
$\mathrm{B}(n, p)$	binomial distribution with parameters n and p
$\mathrm{N}(\mu, \sigma^2)$	normal distribution with mean μ and variance σ^2
μ	population mean
σ^2	population variance
σ	population standard deviation
$\bar{x}$	sample mean
s^2	unbiased estimate of population variance from a sample,

$$s^2 = \frac{1}{n-1}\sum(x - \bar{x})^2$$

ϕ	probability density function of the standardised normal variable with distribution $\mathrm{N}(0, 1)$
Φ	corresponding cumulative distribution function
α, β	regression coefficients
ρ	product-moment correlation coefficient for a population
r	product-moment correlation coefficient for a sample
$\sim p$	not p
$p \Rightarrow q$	p implies q (if p then q)
$p \Leftrightarrow q$	p implies and is implied by q (p is equivalent to q)

Index